Gardening with Nature

Gardening with Nature
at the New York Botanical Garden

PHOTOGRAPHS BY Larry Lederman

TEXT BY Todd A. Forrest

FOREWORD BY Jennifer Bernstein

M

Contents

The New York Botanical Garden is located in the ancestral homeland of the Lenape (Delaware) people. We honor them and acknowledge their displacement, dispossession, and continued presence.

Foreword

JENNIFER BERNSTEIN

CEO & The William C. Steere Sr. President, New York Botanical Garden

IN THE FOLLOWING PAGES, you will learn about the New York Botanical Garden's commitment to and journey toward gardening *with* nature. Implicit in this idea is the recognition that people and nature are not separate. People are a part, perhaps too dominant a part, of every ecosystem in which they live. We simply cannot separate ourselves from nature. This is the reason that we seek communion with nature when we want to feel more connected and embodied, and it is the reason that so many of us find joy in the quiet of the garden. While this inextricable link can be a source of great happiness and solace, we must also confront the dire consequences of our unchecked influence on nature, evidenced by the dual climate and biodiversity crises.

This reframing of our relationship to nature has the potential for profound healing, at both the individual and planetary scale. To see ourselves as part of nature means that we have a responsibility to it and that its well-being will necessarily improve our own. It also means releasing the false sense of control that has dominated our mental structures. Importantly, this shift in thinking allows us to take full advantage of the skills and talents that have long been demonstrated by the best gardeners.

A drift of betony pokes through a matrix of prairie dropseed in the Azalea Garden.

Gardeners may have specialties in specific plants or styles, but there are a few characteristics that cut across. The first is that gardeners are keen observers. They are paying close attention to the places under their care. This slow, deliberate, and careful observation is what lends gardening some of the meditative quality that so many enjoy. We rush about our lives missing much of the detail, but not so in the garden. Gardeners are also responsive to changing conditions. Is that ground saturated? Are the temperatures getting warmer or cooler? Is the soil healthy and nitrogen rich? The conditions of the garden change every day, and the best gardeners are responding in kind. Finally, excellent gardeners have an ecosystem mindset. They consider the role of each plant in relationship with the others and with the insects, birds, and others in the environment. They know that their actions in the garden impact the local fauna and the quality of the air and water. Through their actions, they are making positive change in the ecosystem in ways small and large.

At NYBG, this reconsideration of our relationship to nature writ large and to the 250-acre landscape that we steward has been the driving force of our modern horticulture program, as you will see beautifully rendered in both words and images here. We believe that by gardening with nature, we can demonstrate the unique beauty and rewards that can come through this sensitive, nuanced, and ecosystem-minded approach.

This shift in mindset is important and necessary. The world needs us to slow down, pay attention, and consider how our actions impact all the life around us. Through gardening with nature, we can do just that.

A sweetgum frames a Katsura tree in its autumn glory.

Gardening with Nature

IMAGINE A GARDEN.

Do you picture tidy beds bursting with flowers that open continuously from last to first frost? Exotic fruits ripening on the vine? Soft and welcoming lawns? Expertly clipped hedges? The shade cast from a single tree? Wherever your mind travels, it is likely that it arrives at a place of beneficence and bounty that lies at the intersection of human creativity and nature's spontaneity. The gardens of our imagination are neither completely artificial, nor completely natural. They channel nature's charm, but they exclude its agency.

From nature's perspective, gardens have not always been as beneficent as we might imagine. From the walled oases of ancient Persia to the hills and ponds of *tsukiyama* gardens of Kyoto, Japan, to the bosquets, allées, and parterres of seventeenth-century Europe, to the picturesque landscapes of eighteenth- and nineteenth-century England, to the suburban lawns of twentieth-century America, the history of gardens has been as much about interrupting nature as it has been about celebrating it.

In our own time, the climate and biodiversity crises have spurred a rethinking of the relationship between gardens and nature. The use of native plants in gardens of all sizes

One of the many striking rock outcrops found across NYBG.

and styles, which has ebbed and flowed in popularity in America since the beginning of the twentieth century, is encouraged and celebrated from coast to coast. Writers such as Douglas Tallamy, an entomologist, and Robin Wall Kimmerer, a botanist and ecologist, have helped gardeners see their landscapes as havens of biodiversity connected to the larger ecosystem. Contemporary landscape architects, including Kate Orff and Michael van Valkenburgh, consider the ecological services provided by the landscapes they design just as much as they do their beauty or human utility.

This nature-focused movement in landscape design is changing the way we alter our environments on all scales, from suburban backyards to city parks to massive public works. Serious gardeners are thinking about bloom sequence from pollinators' perspectives as well as their own. Municipalities are investing in street trees and parks as green infrastructure to mitigate the impacts of climate change. Even the Army Corps of Engineers, best known for the prodigious use of concrete in the construction of dams, levees, and canals, is planting vast wetlands to treat stormwater runoff in a signature project of the Comprehensive Everglades Restoration Plan in south Florida. We are collectively beginning to recognize that gardening with nature, on every scale, might be our best hope for a future as fruitful as our past.

The principles of gardening with nature are simple. Garden-makers should take time to understand the biotic (all the living things within the location) and abiotic (the physical characteristics of the site, including climate, geology, topography, hydrology elevation, and soils) conditions of the site. They should strive to fully understand how the plants and the built elements of the garden might take advantage of those biotic and abiotic conditions and how they might damage or interrupt them. Garden-makers should consider their garden as part of, not separate from, the larger environment. Anything planted or applied in a garden is added to an ecosystem, not just to a place. They should take into account the resources required to build and maintain the garden. This last point is often missed in even the most nature-sensitive garden design. A garden designed without regard for the resources necessary for its care is doomed to fail aesthetically and ecologically.

Just as there are many reasons to make a garden and many styles of gardening, there are many ways to garden with nature. A nature-friendly garden does not need to be an ersatz natural area devoid of structures or flourishes intended to accommodate or delight people. It can be formal or naturalistic or both. While it should include as many regionally native plants as possible—preferably chosen to attract and sustain birds, butterflies, bees, and other wildlife—it need not be limited to native plants. It should be planted and maintained in a way that does not impair the air, water, or local flora and fauna. Most of all, it should give the gardener joy. What is a garden if not a joyful place?

Gardening with nature provides joy without harming the larger environment. This approach will be a fundamental part of our collective efforts to repair some of the damage we

Late-winter sun illuminates the layered plantings of the Rock Garden, established by T. H. Everett in 1932.

have already done to the ecosystems that sustain us. Ambitious restoration projects such as the one underway in the Everglades combine modern ecosystem science with traditional horticultural techniques to reestablish native plant and animal biodiversity and ecosystem function on a large scale. Douglas Tallamy's Homegrown National Park movement achieves scale by connecting the efforts of individual gardeners across the country who are actively designing and planting their own gardens to support and sustain wild plants and animals. The Audubon Society, Nature Conservancy, and other national conservation organizations similarly encourage gardeners to put their passion to work on behalf of the larger environment. Recognizing that people will have to play an active role in reversing the environmental degradation that we have caused, the United Nations named 2021–2030 the Decade on Ecosystem Restoration. It is clear that we will have to garden our way out of the climate and biodiversity crises we have created.

Nathaniel Britton (fourth from right) and the Scientific Directors break ground for the Library Building on New Year's Eve, 1899. MERTZ LIBRARY, NYBG.

We have learned a great deal about gardening with nature at the New York Botanical Garden (NYBG). An appreciation for, and deference to, nature shaped the institution's mission during its founding in 1891, and those principles have guided its development since the selection of its site in the Bronx in 1895. This nature-first ethos is in part a reflection of the era in which NYBG was created, the convictions of its founders Nathaniel and Elizabeth Britton, and the collective will of generations of botanists, educators, and horticulturists who have carried out NYBG's mission since its founding.

Modeled after the Royal Botanic Garden at Kew in London, NYBG was established by an act of the New York State Legislature in 1891 to pursue a three-part mission of scientific research, education about nature and plants, and horticultural display. It was the third (after the American Museum of Natural History and the Metropolitan Museum of Art) of the great New York City cultural institutions created in the nineteenth and early twentieth centuries through partnerships between Gilded Age philanthropists and civic leaders who recognized that great cities need vibrant culture as well as robust commerce.

A commitment to nature-sensitive gardening has shaped NYBG's landscape from the late nineteenth-century layout of the living plant collections assembled to serve the institution's research and educational missions to the recent development of a suite of new gardens and collections designed to engage and delight visitors. In every era, NYBG has centered and celebrated nature while also building its living collections in support of its mission, responding to changing horticultural tastes, and addressing evolving concerns about how this, and every, garden fits within its larger ecological context.

Over time, gardening with nature at NYBG has created an urban landscape that features well-cared-for and ecologically robust natural areas, diverse living plant collections, and traditional and modern approaches to garden design while preserving a consistent and compelling sense of place. It is a landscape that can inspire anyone with an interest in developing a garden, on any scale, that satisfies the human urge to create a place of beneficence and bounty while also contributing to efforts to reverse the damage we have done to our planet.

This book explores NYBG's commitment to gardening with nature through images of and essays on the natural landscapes, plant collections, and display gardens that best reflect this commitment. They range from the 50-acre Thain Family Forest, which inspired the selection of the site in 1895, to the Native Plant Garden, which opened in 2013 and combines sustainable materials and construction techniques with artfully arranged plantings of our regional flora. Although NYBG is fortunate to employ the most skilled horticulturists in the world, the nature-friendly plants and gardening techniques featured here are accessible to any home gardener, from beginner to expert, interested in joining the effort to heal our planet one plant at a time.

Larry Lederman, who has spent more than two decades exploring NYBG with his camera, spent several years photographing these gardens and landscapes in all seasons and all weather. His pictures capture the results of NYBG's history of nature-sensitive gardening better than any words ever could.

The New York Botanical Garden is an oasis of nature within the dense urban sprawl of New York City. MARLON CO, NYBG.

New York Botanical Garden

THE GARDEN'S FOUNDERS, including founding director Nathaniel Britton (1859–1934), his wife, botanist Elizabeth Britton (1858–1934), and a board of trustees made up of prominent, civic-minded New Yorkers, imagined a great scientific institution dedicated to shedding light on the mysteries of the plant world, an educational institution where students of all ages and backgrounds could learn about the wonders of plants, and an urban green space that would provide an escape from the tumult of the surrounding city. While they looked to Kew and other urban European botanic gardens for inspiration for the scientific and educational roots of their new institution, the Brittons also recognized that they had an opportunity to create a uniquely American institution that combined scientific and educational pursuits with social benefits including access to nature for all city residents.

The 1891 Act of Incorporation authorized NYBG to select 250 acres of parkland in the Bronx, the northernmost borough of New York City, once the inchoate institution raised $250,000 (about $9 million in 2024 dollars) to support the development of its programs and collections.[1] In early 1895, Nathaniel Britton and NYBG's Scientific Directors, a committee of experts that included Seth Low (1850–1916), President of Columbia University; Addison Brown (1830–1913), a Federal judge and a respected botanist; Columbia geologist

The Bronx River and Thain Family Forest are the wild heart of the NYBG historic landscape.

James Kemp (1859–1926), chemist Charles Chandler (1836–1925), and others, toured several locations in the Bronx searching for a site that would support NYBG's ambitious plans. The funds were largely in hand by May of that year, and in June 1895, NYBG announced that it had chosen the northern half of Bronx Park as its home.

Bronx Park was part of nearly 3,500 acres of parkland set aside by the New Parks Act of 1884 and purchased by New York City between 1888 and 1890. The site, one of three Britton and the Scientific Directors considered for NYBG's home, had been owned by generations of the Lorillard Family from 1792 until Pierre Lorillard IV sold it to New York City. The landscape was remarkable for its natural beauty. At its heart was a dense old-growth hemlock-hardwood forest known as the "Hemlock Grove," which was bisected by the dramatic gorge and rushing rapids of the Bronx River, New York City's only freshwater river, which the Lorillards dammed to power the mill they used to grind tobacco into snuff. Surrounding the forest were fertile fields and pastures shaded by ancient native trees. The topography was dramatically varied, with more than 100 feet of elevation change between the highest ridges of gneiss and schist and the lowest seeps of protected valleys. Evidence of glaciation was everywhere in the form of glacial erratic boulders, bedrock striations, and potholes carved into solid rock.

This wild site on the edge of the expanding city could not have been more different from the great British and European botanic gardens that served as inspiration for NYBG's

Above: Nathaniel Britton on a 1905 expedition in the Bahamas. MERTZ LIBRARY, NYBG.
Opposite: Mountain hydrangea thrives in the shade of the Azalea Garden's mature trees.

program of science, education, and horticulture. Hortus Botanicus Leiden was established in 1590 as a walled garden within a university campus in an ancient Dutch city. The Jardin des Plantes was created in 1635 on the grounds of a chateau within the formal urban grid of Paris. Kew was established in 1840 on a former royal estate on the flat topography of the Thames floodplain in London. While NYBG's founders shared these institutions' commitment to research, education, and the cultivation and display of diverse collections of the world's plants, the site they chose represented a profound new direction in urban botanical garden design.

NYBG's nature-forward approach to garden building did not end with the choice of a picturesque natural landscape as its home. The only condition written into the transfer agreement was that the Hemlock Grove be preserved in perpetuity—a condition that the founders enthusiastically accepted.[2] In addition to protecting the forest, Britton and John Brinley (1861–1946), a landscape engineer who worked with Britton to create the 1896 *General Plan for the New York Botanical Garden,*[3] made every effort to arrange the plant collections to support the research and educational missions in a way that preserved and incorporated the thousands of ancient native trees on the site.

The choice of site and plans for NYBG's development captured the attention of leaders of other American botanical gardens and arboreta, particularly Charles Sprague Sargent (1841–1927), the founding director of the Arnold Arboretum of Harvard University. Sargent

Above: An 1899 image of some of the many mature native trees preserved during NYBG's development.
Opposite: The 1896 *General Plan* protected the Bronx River, Hemlock Grove, and other natural areas across the landscape.
MERTZ LIBRARY, NYBG.

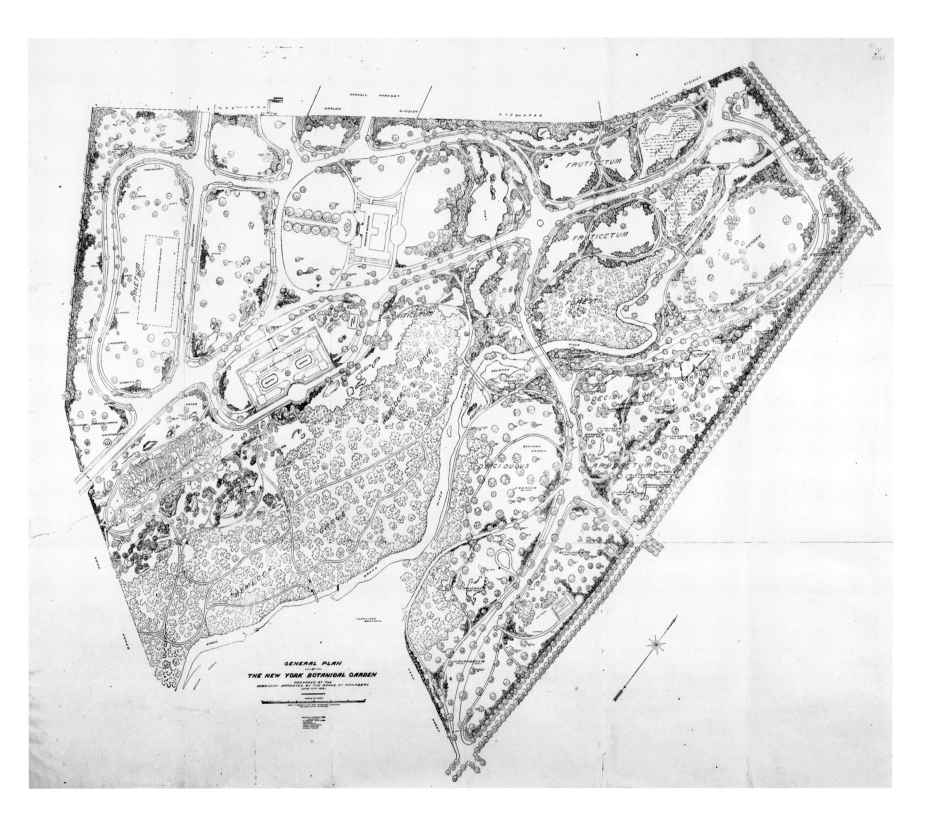

GENERAL PLAN
OF
THE NEW YORK BOTANICAL GARDEN
PREPARED BY THE
COMMISSION APPOINTED BY THE BOARD OF MANAGERS
JUNE 11TH 1896

recognized the enormous scientific, educational, and aesthetic advantage of a botanical garden built around an old-growth urban forest and took great interest in plans for the site. Sargent's interest became public when, concerned about the location Britton and Brinley had chosen for the expansive conservatory that was to house the tropical plant collections, he published an editorial in the journal *Garden and Forest* on June 30, 1897:

> No city in the world possesses more beautiful scenery or a park area more thoroughly characteristic of what is most delightful in the landscape of the part of the world in which it is situated than does New York in Bronx Park. There seems to be some danger that a portion of it which has been handed over to the directors of the Botanical Garden may be marred by the intrusion of buildings which could be placed elsewhere. Let us hope that conservative counsel will prevent any such desecration. The city spent money like water to create some charming natural scenery in what is now Central Park by blasting out ridges of rock, filling in the spaces with soil, and turning this desert of stone into tree-flecked meadow-land. Now that it has come into possession of scenery far more beautiful and ready-made, it would be worse than folly to destroy it.[4]

The Garden's founders were intent on preserving the natural beauty Sargent extolled so eloquently, but they understood they would need to create buildings and infrastructure to support the research and education programs. They knew they would have to plant diverse living collections of exotic plants to serve the mission as a botanical garden. They made every effort to achieve the program in concert with the compelling nature of the site, setting aside about 85 acres of natural areas and placing buildings and aligning roads and paths to avoid damaging the ancient oaks (*Quercus* spp.), maples (*Acer* spp.), hickories (*Carya* spp.), elms (*Ulmus* spp.), and other native trees that grew spontaneously across the landscape.

NYBG founders aligned the Garden's roads to preserve the many native trees that grew across the site. MERTZ LIBRARY, NYBG.

NYBG educators and scientists took advantage of the site's bounteous nature. The very first educational activity was the labeling of the native trees preserved during construction.[5] One of the first scientific articles published in the *Bulletin of The New York Botanical Garden* was an 1897 study of the geologic origins of the Bronx River gorge by James Kemp.[6] In 1898 and 1899, Nathaniel Britton and George Nash (1864–1921), NYBG's head gardener, cataloged the flora of the site, documenting 336 native and 76 naturalized species growing spontaneously within the boundaries.[7] The choice of a site so richly endowed with natural features bore immediate educational and scientific fruit.

The natural features of the landscape were also instrumental in the development of one of the world's first plant conservation organizations—the Wildflower Preservation Society of America (WPS). The WPS was co-founded in 1902 by Elizabeth Britton, Cornell horticulturist

This grove of sweet gum,
pin oak, and white oak near
the LuEsther T. Mertz Library
predates NYBG's establishment.

Liberty Hyde Bailey (1858–1954), botanist Alice Eastwood (1859–1953), and others. Within a few years of the Garden's opening, Britton observed the rapid decline of wildflower populations in the forest and other natural areas as they were picked or trampled by visitors. She surmised that if such a decline could occur so quickly under the watchful eye of NYBG botanists, it could occur anywhere. She continued to advocate for the conservation of wildflowers until her death in 1934. Although the Wildflower Preservation Society of America disbanded in 1933, its spirit lives on in contemporary organizations devoted to protecting the native plants of America, including the Lady Bird Johnson Wildflower Center, the Native Plant Trust, the California Native Plant Society, and many others.

The Brittons' passion for preserving nature became embedded in the spirit of the place and the people who care for it. In 1967 the National Park Service designated the Garden a National Historic Landmark, citing the beauty of its natural landscape and acknowledging that even with "the evolution of an active program, the appearance of the Garden is still essentially that of its youth."[8] Nearly every major landscape project completed at NYBG has been undertaken with sensitivity to the exceptional natural beauty that inspired the selection of a particularly wild and dramatic portion of Bronx Park as the Garden's home. In each era, the NYBG garden-makers have applied different tools and techniques to address the challenges and opportunities of their day, but always with an eye to preserving the nature of the site. With the exception of the suite of gardens immediately adjacent to the Enid A. Haupt Conservatory, which were designed to respond to the architecture of that grand building, even our more formal or highly constructed gardens, such as the Peggy Rockefeller Rose Garden and the Edible Academy, have been designed to sit gently within

Wamsler Rock, a glacially sculpted rock outcrop near the entrance to the Rock Garden.

the natural landscape. Of course, there have been some horticultural interventions over time that have missed the mark, but these ultimately faded away, while the Garden's more nature-sensitive features have persevered.

Since 1998, we have been working to restore and revitalize the NYBG landscape with the goals of engaging modern audiences, improving accessibility, and addressing the challenges presented by the changing climate. We have substantially improved about 150 acres so far, and we have plans to keep on going until it is time to start again. This has been the most active period in our history since the initial construction of buildings, roads, and living collections between 1895 and 1915. Our work has been guided by an abiding appreciation for NYBG's history, a desire to captivate our visitors, and a growing conviction that nature-inspired gardening is best for both people and the planet. With the support of visionary philanthropists, a dedicated team of senior leaders, particularly Gregory Long, who led NYBG from 1989 to 2018, horticulturists, educators, and project managers partnered with some of our era's most talented designers to conceive and complete this work. The landscapes and gardens featured here (by no means a complete list of all we have done or NYBG has to offer), which Larry Lederman has captured so beautifully, show how a visit to NYBG in any season will reveal how satisfying and uplifting gardening with nature can be.

Above: Cutting hay the old-fashioned way in September 1917. MERTZ LIBRARY, NYBG.
Opposite: The Native Plant Garden water feature follows the contours of the land. MARLON CO, NYBG.

Above: The massive trunk of a
venerable red oak.
Opposite: The Stone Mill,
constructed by the Lorillard
Family in 1840, is a National
Historic Landmark.

Above: This large rock outcrop
was smoothed by glaciers.
Right: "Split Rock" is a large
boulder of Yonkers Gneiss
deposited on the site during
the last Ice Age.

The Stone Mill Dam was
constructed by the Lorillards in
the nineteenth century to power
the Stone Mill.

Thain Family Forest and
the Bronx River

The most notable natural feature of the Botanical Garden, perhaps as a matter of botany and certainly as a matter of landscape, is the gorge of the Bronx River with its wild growth of hemlocks and associated plants, its picturesque precipitous slopes and ledges, its sense of remoteness and seclusion from the city and most of the works of men.[9]

—Olmsted Brothers, 1924

THE THAIN FAMILY FOREST is the largest remnant of the woodlands that once covered most of what is now New York City. Never cleared for agriculture or industry, it has been continuously forested since our region's vegetation transitioned from post-glacial tundra to boreal conifers approximately 13,000 years ago.[10] It serves as a natural buffer for the Bronx River, which flows for nearly a mile through NYBG's landscape on its 23-mile course from northern Westchester County to the East River. The forest and the river were within the territory of the Lenape people for thousands of years before the arrival of the first Europeans in the 1600s. Following the forced displacement of the Lenape by Dutch

The flowering of our native red maple marks the beginning of spring.

and English colonists, the land was included in various large estates. Fortunately, each successive generation of landowners preserved these invaluable natural areas as New York City grew around them.

Prior to NYBG's founding, the Forest, then called the Hemlock Grove because of its stands of mature eastern hemlock (*Tsuga canadensis*), was a prized natural area at the edge of the expanding city. In his 1818 poem *Bronx*, Joseph Rodman Drake (1795–1820) noted its "dark cedars with loose mossy tresses." Paintings by Hudson River School artists Samuel Robinson Gifford (1823–1880) and William Rickarby Miller (1818–1893) depicted its towering trees reflected in the waters of the Bronx River. In a 1905 lecture to the Bronx Academy of Arts and Sciences, Nathaniel Britton quoted William E. Dodge Jr. (1832–1903), a prominent New Yorker and founding trustee of the Garden, who described the Forest as "the most precious natural possession of the city of New York."[11]

Every generation of NYBG's leadership has strived to preserve the natural beauty of the Forest and the Bronx River. As the scientific understanding of natural ecosystems has changed, so has the approach to stewardship. At the time of NYBG's founding, scientists believed that forested ecosystems in a given region developed in a predictable progression from initial establishment to maturity. In this view of forest development, or succession, forests dominated by long-lived, shade-tolerant species such as hemlock were considered to have reached the final, or climax, stage of development and would remain stable unless impacted by a significant disturbance such as a fire or hurricane. Since the NYBG Forest included stands of ancient hemlocks, Britton and his contemporaries believed that it had reached the climax stage and therefore the best approach to its stewardship was a policy of "let alone."[12] They believed that any direct human intervention in the Forest would diminish it.

A 1909 photograph of one of the forest paths that allowed early NYBG visitors to immerse themselves in nature. MERTZ LIBRARY, NYBG.

Within only a few years of NYBG's founding, Britton's perspective on intervening in the Forest changed. The 1904 discovery of chestnut blight, an introduced fungal pest from Asia, in the Bronx Zoo, which is adjacent to NYBG, ultimately led to the removal of American chestnut (*Castanea dentata*) from the Forest. In 1906, concerned about fires and the "indiscriminate trampling" of the forest soils by crowds, Britton considered installing fences along the trails.[13] In the early 1920s, during a comparative ecological study of hemlock forests at NYBG, in Connecticut, and in the Adirondacks, NYBG scientists noted that there were fewer hemlock seedlings in the NYBG Forest compared with similar sites, likely caused by soil compaction and trampling by visitors.[14] This study ultimately inspired the planting of hemlock saplings in the Forest in 1925 and 1926.

The change from a policy of "let alone" to one of active management came at a time when our understanding of natural ecosystems was itself changing. Henry Gleason (1882–1975), NYBG scientist and one of the authors of the hemlock study, was a leading figure in the development of a new perspective of how ecosystems function and change.

Left: The old mill race along the
Bronx River has been converted
into an accessible path.
Opposite: Simple post and rail
fences protect forest soil from
compaction by the wandering
feet of visitors.

He argued that complex interactions between individual species drive the development of ecosystems over time and that the concept of stable climax ecosystems was fundamentally flawed. To Gleason, ecosystems were dynamic assemblages of species interacting with their abiotic environment and each other.

More than a century of observation in the Thain Family Forest has shown that the interaction between humans and other species may well be the most profound ecological interaction of all. Chestnut blight and soil compaction were just the start. A study in the early 1980s showed that the population of eastern gray squirrels was exceedingly high, in part due to feeding by visitors. These ravenous squirrels have had a significant impact on the regeneration of the native oaks and hickories in the Forest. The arrival of the hemlock wooly adelgid, a devastating insect pest of hemlock introduced into North America from Japan, at NYBG in the late 1980s sealed the fate of eastern hemlock, which had not been regenerating successfully since the early 1900s—fewer than 100 living hemlocks stand in the Forest today. As the hemlocks have declined, populations of invasive plants including Amur cork-tree (*Phellodendron amurense*), lesser celandine (*Ficaria verna*), knotweed (*Fallopia* spp.), and porcelain berry (*Ampelopsis brevipedunculata*) have increased. It is clear that, with the presence of these and other human-caused disturbances, simply letting the Forest alone would ultimately lead to its demise.

By the early 2000s, we concluded that active intervention would be necessary to reverse this decades-long ecological decline. With the help of then NYBG trustees Carmen and John Thain, who understood the profound importance of the Forest, we created the Thain Family

We are experimenting with ways to control knotweed, which has become established along the banks of the Bronx River.

It is important to leave fallen trees on the forest floor. They create habitat for native wildlife and provide nutrients that feed the growth of the future forest.

Forest Program in 2008. Its goals are to accommodate access to the Forest for research, education, and enjoyment and to develop and employ ecological restoration practices to address the most pressing human-caused threats to its health. Our first task was to improve the path system, which had deteriorated to the point that visitors would often step off paths to avoid muddy or uneven spots, trampling native plants and compacting the soil. Since we knew that the damage inadvertently caused by visitors had greatly impacted the health of the Forest since the Brittons' time, we retained landscape architects Andropogon Associates to help us redesign and reconstruct the paths to make them more welcoming and easier to maintain. We want as many people as possible to enjoy the Forest without causing it harm.

As we improved access for visitors, we began implementing a program of ecological restoration to address some of the other threats to the health of the Forest. The evolving practice of ecological restoration is part ecological science and part gardening. Ecological science provides the framework to understand which plant communities should be present in an ecosystem and how those communities should function together with pollinators, seed dispersers, and other living things. Ecological restorationists typically identify a reference period at some point in the past and establish strategies to recreate the plant and animal communities of that period. Often, ecological restoration projects begin with the removal of invasive plant species and proceed with the planting of native plants grown from locally or regionally collected seeds.

Our approach to the ecological restoration of the Thain Family Forest aligns with this typical practice, although it differs in some very important ways. The Forest, which has

The brilliant fall foliage of a red maple stands out against the russet tones of oaks.

never been cleared and has evolved (more or less) naturally since the end of the last glacial period, is very different from the second- or third-growth forests that are typically the subjects of ecological restoration efforts in our region. Most of these forests have regrown on land cleared for agriculture, are dominated by trees that are all about the same age, and often include dense stands of common invasive plants such as Norway maple (*Acer platanoides*), Japanese barberry (*Berberis thunbergii*), or burning bush (*Euonymus alatus*). They require substantial intervention to re-establish native plant species and the ecological processes that enable them to become self-sustaining. In many ways, restoring such forests is very similar to restarting the successional processes that created them in the first place and requires clearing, regular herbicide applications, and massive planting efforts to establish desirable species.

The Thain Family Forest is different. It is a mosaic of trees of various ages ranging from seedlings that sprouted last year to centuries-old titans. It is dominated by long-lived, late-successional native trees such as sugar maple (*Acer saccharum*), American beech (*Fagus grandifolia*), tulip tree (*Liriodendron tulipifera*), sweet gum (*Liquidambar styraciflua*), and seven different native oaks. Only two native tree species that were once abundant on the site are effectively missing—American chestnut and eastern hemlock. Since both of these species have been decimated by introduced pests, neither can be effectively reestablished until those pests have been extirpated from our region. At best, efforts to reestablish them would be an exercise in futility. At worst, it would require a commitment to regular applications of pesticides for generations to come.

The banks of the Bronx River are lined by dense forest along its entire course through NYBG.

Left and above: The shallow,
rocky soils that characterize
much of the Thain Family
Forest make its trees prone
to uprooting in windstorms.
Overleaf: Split-rail fencing
borders the path.

Since the tree canopy of the Thain Family Forest is and has always been composed primarily of native species, we do not need to look to the past to guide our restoration activities. Instead, we work to promote the natural regeneration of the native tree species that have proved to be adapted to site conditions as they are today rather than as they were four hundred years ago. We do this primarily by removing invasive species from canopy gaps where native trees have fallen and replanting these gaps with native species grown from locally collected seed. We also monitor for emerging threats to the health of the Forest and address them as necessary. Every year brings new threats—since the Thain Family Forest program began in 2008, we have had to contend with Italian arum (*Arum italicum*), Japanese stilt grass (*Microstegium vimineum*) and other new invasive plants; emerald ash borer (*Agrilus planipennis*), spotted lanternfly (*Lycorma delicatula*) and other new insect pests; and beech leaf disease (*Litylenchus crenatae mccannii*), bacterial leaf scorch of oaks (*Xylella fastidiosa*), and other new diseases. Our experience has shown us that with thoughtful intervention, the natural processes that created the Forest will sustain it, even in the face of significant human-caused disturbance.

We instituted a continuous forest inventory project in 2002 to inform our management activities and track our progress. Every five years we identify and measure all the trees >= 1 cm diameter-at-breast-height in a set of 249 10-by-10-meter research plots that represent an approximately 15 percent sample of the Forest's entire area.[15] While the plots were initially installed to track the Forest's trees, we began sampling herbaceous plants in 2011 to better understand how climate change and other anthropogenic disturbances are impacting populations of native ferns, wildflowers, and other herbaceous plants. Data

Early fall along the Bronx River.

Winter is the best time to see the complex structure of the Thain Family Forest, which includes a mix of mature trees that have grown on the site for centuries and younger trees that represent the forest of the future.

from the continuous forest inventory have shown that our management of invasive species is having a positive impact. Amur cork tree, which increased in abundance between 2002 and 2006, has declined substantially since we began managing it aggressively in 2008. The planting of native trees in canopy gaps formed during Sandy, Isaias, Ida, and other severe storms has prevented re-invasion of Amur cork tree and the spread of other invasive tree species. In the coming years, we will develop protocols for reestablishing populations of some of the ferns and wildflowers that once thrived in the Forest but have diminished or disappeared over time.

The natural beauty of the Forest and Bronx River inspired the choice of NYBG's site in 1895 and set it apart from other urban botanical gardens around the world. This nature-first spirit also profoundly influenced the initial design of the landscape and living collections and has informed the evolution of NYBG's horticultural features since 1895. Over the same period, the anthropogenic climate and biodiversity crises have significantly impacted the health of the Forest. While we once thought the best approach to preserving the nature of the Forest was to leave it alone, we know now that we must intervene in order to mitigate the negative human influences that threaten its health. We have learned that the fundamental skills of horticulture, once considered out of place in the Forest, will be required to save it. It is our hope that our work in the Thain Family Forest will inspire stewards of natural areas in New York and beyond to engage in active restoration before it is too late.

Unlike many forests in the region, which are plagued by deer, the Thain Family Forest has a rich understory flora.

Right: A healthy forest has many layers of vegetation.
Overleaf: Vernal pools provide essential habitat for salamanders,
which thrive in the Forest.

The well-oxygenated rocky shallows of the Bronx River gorge create habitat for a variety of aquatic organisms.

Daffodil Hill

IN AN 1896 LECTURE about the origins and evolution of botanical gardens, Nathaniel Britton stated that "the rectilinear treatment of plant beds found in most of the older gardens has become abhorrent to landscape lovers," and, therefore, the plantings in botanical gardens should "follow, as nearly as possible, a natural treatment."[16] Britton and Brinley's *General Plan* reflected this design philosophy. About 85 acres of forest, river, swamps, meadows, and other natural areas were set aside as nature reserves, and about 125 acres of arable land outside the Forest were allocated for plant collections arranged according to their evolutionary relationships for educational purposes. Purely decorative plantings were restricted to the 25 acres set aside for buildings.

This arrangement was sympathetic to the natural features of the site and provided both ample growing space for the collections and convenient access for students and scientists to study them. However, it did not leave much room for showcasing the burgeoning field of ornamental horticulture. This initial lack of emphasis on the art of gardening did not appear to cause concern among NYBG's early advocates, but it gradually became a point of contention as ornamental gardening grew in popularity in the United States, fueled by the writings of British garden writers William Robinson (1838–1935) and Gertrude Jekyll (1843–1932) and a boom in garden-making in the wealthy suburbs of America's cities. By

Daffodil Hill in 1933, nearly a decade after the first *Narcissus* bulbs were planted. MERTZ LIBRARY, NYBG.

the early 1900s, American garden designers, including Beatrix Farrand (1872–1959), Marian

Coffin (1876–1957), and Ellen Shipman (1869–1950), all based in New York, were creating

magnificent gardens across the country that rivaled those of their British counterparts. In

1913 a group of civic-minded women established the Garden Club of America, a coalition

of garden clubs from across the country, to elevate the art of gardening in America.

Members of the Women's Auxiliary, a committee established to advise the then all-

male Board of Managers in 1914, were early advocates for augmenting NYBG's natural

landscape and systematically arranged plant collections with horticultural features

designed as much for beauty as for science and education. The inaugural committee

included a number of women who had substantial gardens in New York State: Mrs.

Thomas H. Barber (Claverack in Southampton), Mrs. James L. Breese (The Orchard in

Southampton), Mrs. Henry Marquand (White Gates Farm in Bedford Hills), and Mrs. James

Roosevelt (Springwood in Hyde Park), among others. These women felt that a botanical

garden of NYBG's global stature should showcase sophisticated and beautiful horticultural

features as well as scientifically arranged plant collections.

The opportunity to add more beautiful horticultural features came soon after the Women's

Auxiliary was convened. In 1915 the Garden annexed approximately 140 acres of land

adjacent to its southern border, increasing its overall size to nearly 400 acres. This new

land featured a quarter mile of frontage along the Bronx River, patches of wetlands and

remnant forest, a lake, and fertile fields perfect for the development of new garden

features. By 1920 the expanded landscape boasted an iris garden, a rose garden

Keating Hall at Fordham University rises above Daffodil Hill.

Crabapples along the edge of
Daffodil Hill add winter structure
and late spring flowers.

designed by Farrand, a small rock garden, groves of flowering trees, plantations of conifers, and a five-acre "horticultural garden" created for the 1917 annual convention of the Society of American Florists and Ornamental Horticulturists.

In 1924 Ethel Anson Peckham (1879–1965), an accomplished botanical artist, horticulturist, and founding member of the American Iris Society, joined the Women's Auxiliary and got to work building NYBG's displays of flowers, particularly iris (*Iris* spp.) and daffodil (*Narcissus* spp.). With about thirty-five species native to moist meadows and open woodlands in the Mediterranean regions of Europe and Northern Africa, daffodils are well suited to New York's climate and perfect for planting naturalistically in open lawns. They are long-lived and require little care other than occasional division and fertilization. Daffodils also lend themselves to hybridization. Horticulturists have bred and named more than 26,000 cultivated varieties, ranging from demure miniatures to stout-stemmed trumpets.

Peckham established a daffodil fund and solicited bulb contributions from the Dutch Bulb Growers Society. Between 1924 and 1925, she oversaw the planting of more than 60,000 daffodil bulbs representing 146 different cultivated varieties on sun-drenched, south-facing slopes adjacent to the Horticultural Garden. The site was ideal for growing daffodils— photographs taken within a few years of the initial plantings show a sea of white and yellow flowers spreading across the landscape as far as the eye can see.

As Peckham was building the daffodil display on Daffodil Hill, as the area came to be known, NYBG horticulturists were planting flowering trees nearby. In a 1924 report on

Left: Crabapples come into full flower toward the end of daffodil season.
Overleaf: A mix of daffodil varieties provides a range of flower colors, shapes, and sizes.

the Garden commissioned by the NYBG trustees, Olmsted Brothers, run by Frederick Law Olmsted's sons, John (1852–1920) and Frederick Jr. (1870–1957), advised planting flowering trees along the perimeter to draw visitors to the Garden in spring.[17] Over the next twenty years, NYBG horticulturists added groves of hawthorn (*Crataegus* spp.), flowering cherry (*Prunus* spp.), flowering pear (*Pyrus* spp.), and crabapple (*Malus* spp.) to Daffodil Hill and adjacent areas to create the Garden's most anticipated spring display.

Drifts of *Narcissus* 'White Queen' in 1930. This heirloom variety still thrives on Daffodil Hill today. MERTZ LIBRARY, NYBG.

Changing fortunes and priorities from the 1930s through the 1960s led to substantial changes to the landscape, including the area around Daffodil Hill. The iris garden was moved closer to the Conservatory in the early 1930s. In 1937 about 150 acres of land along the eastern border were taken by New York State for the construction of the Bronx River Parkway, reducing the Garden's total acreage back to 250 acres. The Horticultural Garden was abandoned in the 1940s. The Rose Garden was similarly abandoned in the late 1960s and reestablished closer to the Conservatory in 1972 (only to be rebuilt on its original site in 1988). By the 2000s, of the suite of horticultural features established on Daffodil Hill in the 1920s, only the conifer plantations, flowering trees, and the daffodils remained. Of these features, only the crabapple collections and the Rose Garden had received much curatorial attention in the intervening years.

Fortunately, daffodils thrive with benign neglect. Over the decades, the offspring of the bulbs Peckham planted on Daffodil Hill persisted and flowered year after year with no care or augmentation. In 2015, on the eve of the 125th anniversary of NYBG's founding, we picked up where Peckham had left off ninety years before and began the Million Daffodil project. Our goal was to add a million new bulbs to complement the descendants of Peckham's original plantings.

Narcissus 'Queen of the North' is another heirloom daffodil that has survived since the 1920s.
CLAIRE LYMAN, NYBG.

This project was led by Kristin Schleiter (1963–2022), curator of outdoor gardens from 2008 to 2018. She began by surveying the daffodils that remained from the original plantings to ensure that the new plantings would blend well with the forms and colors of the heirloom varieties that had persisted. She then worked with Brent Heath and Jay Hutchins of Brent and Becky's Bulbs in Gloucester, Virginia, to source modern cultivars adapted to the site. In the fall of 2015, we used a special bulb planting machine from Holland to plant 150,000 bulbs of ten different daffodil cultivars, including several introduced by legendary daffodil breeder William Pannill (1927–2014).

Plantings have continued every year since 2015, with an emphasis on filling in gaps in the display. In 2019 associate curator Claire Lyman began identifying and documenting the heirloom cultivars planted by Peckham. Through painstaking research in the NYBG

Above left: *Narcissus* 'Ice Follies'. Above right: *Narcissus* 'Chromacolor'. Two of the new daffodil varieties added to Daffodil Hill since 2015.
CLAIRE LYMAN, NYBG.
Right: Daffodil Hill in peak flower in mid-April.

archives and countless hours in the field, Lyman identified nearly thirty varieties that remain from the historic plantings, including 'Conspicuus', 'St. Olaf', 'Firebrand', 'Sir Watkin', Queen of the North', and 'White Queen', and photographed many more that still await positive identification. In recent years, we have focused on digging, dividing, and replanting these heirloom cultivars to ensure that they will continue to survive. The combination of the historic plants and the new bulbs creates a breathtaking display that begins with the cheerful yellow flowers of 'Rapture', which open toward the end of March, and ends with the elegant white flowers of the pheasant's eye daffodil (*Narcissus poeticus* var. *recurvus*), which can still be in flower as late as the first week of May.

Tough, beautiful, and adaptable, daffodils are the perfect plant for gardeners seeking to garden with nature. They behave in gardens much as they do in their native environments and flower year after year with little specialized care. We allow the foliage to die back before we cut the grass in early July. We fertilize only if the plants show signs of nutrient deficiency. Perhaps most important, daffodils have shown no tendency to become invasive in our natural habitats. While they do not provide much, if any, benefit to native pollinators, they do not appear to do any harm. They do, however, give people joy and bring them closer to nature, as the throngs who have flocked to Daffodil Hill every April since 1925 will attest.

Above: Dividing heirloom daffodils for replanting on Daffodil Hill.
Opposite: Allowing the daffodil foliage to die back before cutting the grass gives the bulbs the energy they need to thrive for the long term.

Exposed bedrock lends
character to Daffodil Hill in
all seasons.

The Olmsted Brothers'
suggestion to add flowering
trees to Daffodil Hill and the
surrounding area has paid
dividends for generations.

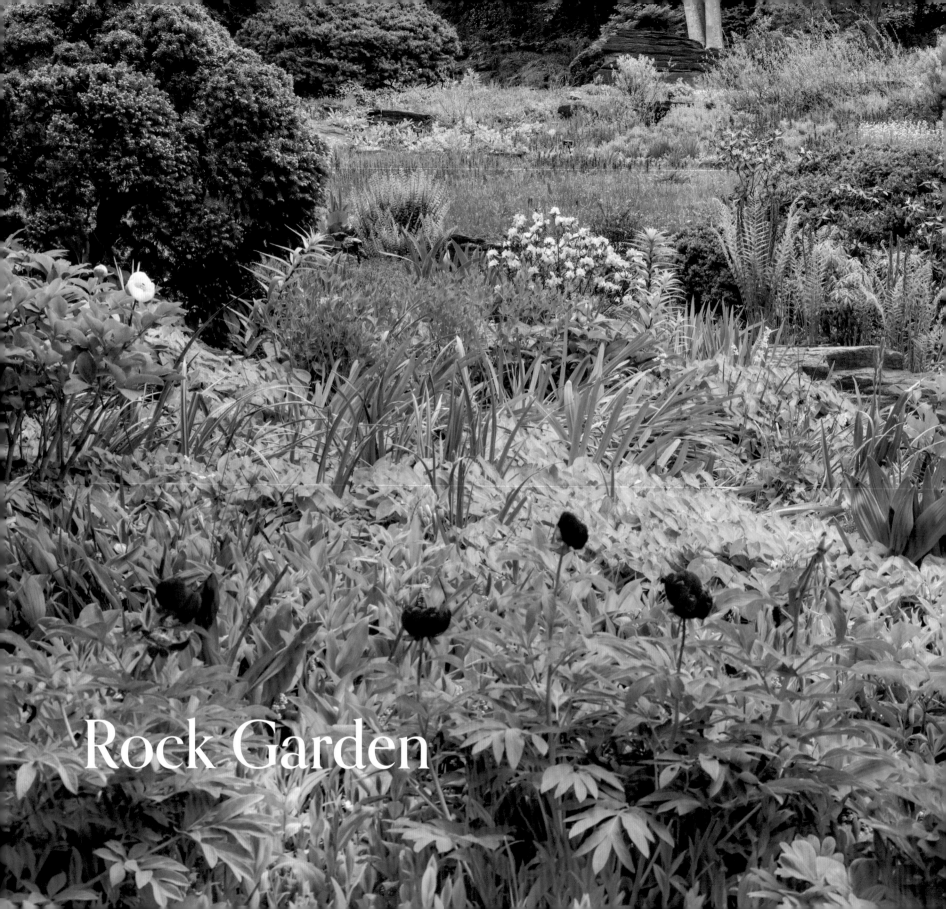

Rock Garden

IF MASSES OF DAFFODILS ARE IDEAL for gardeners who want to complement the natural features of their garden with a splash of laissez-faire spring color, a rock garden is perfectly suited for those who desire to distill the wonders of nature into a horticulturally exacting microcosm. The Rock Garden at NYBG was built between 1932 and 1935 by legendary horticulturist T. H. Everett (1903–1986), who worked in various capacities at NYBG from 1932 until 1967. Born in England and trained at Kew, Everett came to America in 1927 to work as a gardener for Samuel Untermyer (1858–1940) at Greystone, Untermyer's estate on the Hudson River in Yonkers, a small city just north of the Bronx. At Greystone, Untermyer worked with architect William Welles Bosworth and teams of skilled horticulturists to create one of the grandest gardens in America, if not the world, with more than 150 acres of formal, romantic, and naturalistic garden spaces extending from a bluff high above the Hudson nearly to the water's edge. Now part of the Yonkers park system, what remains of Untermyer's remarkable garden is being restored to its former glory.

Horticultural cognoscenti considered rock gardens the apotheosis of fine horticulture during Everett's formative years in England. British horticulturists developed rock gardens, or rockeries, in the late eighteenth century as a way to showcase the botanical

The Rock Garden is one of NYBG's most treasured spring destinations.

treasures plant collectors were bringing back from expeditions to far-flung alpine regions. Bellflowers (*Campanula* spp.) from the Dalmatians, edelweiss (*Leontopodium nivale*) from the Dolomites, gentians (*Gentiana* spp.) from the Caucasus, primroses (*Primula* spp.) and geraniums (*Geranium* spp.) from the Himalayas, bitterroot (*Lewisia* spp.) from the Bitterroots, and countless other new plants were becoming available to sophisticated gardeners across Britain. Many required highly specific horticultural conditions to thrive, even in the benign climate of the British Isles. Since their native mountain habitats were cool and rocky, it stood to reason that mimicking those conditions in gardens would lead to horticultural success with alpine plants. In 1773 gardeners at the Chelsea Physic Garden in London constructed the Pond Rockery from ships' ballast, building rubble, and even clam shells to provide a suitable habitat for alpine plants.

Rockeries continued to grow in popularity in Britain and across Europe through the Victorian era and into the twentieth century. Not all were dedicated to the cultivation of alpine plants and, as the fashion spread and technology evolved, they became larger and more elaborate. Perhaps the most impressive rockeries were not made from rocks at all; they were created using Pulhamite, an artificial stone similar to concrete invented in the 1820s by James Pulham (1765–1830). Landscape gardeners used Pulhamite to create grottoes, waterfalls, and fantasy mountainscapes at some of England's grandest estates, including Waddeson Manor, built by the Rothschild family in the late 1800s.

In *Alpine Flowers for English Gardens* (1870), William Robinson gave practical and aesthetic advice to would-be rock gardeners. Robinson abhorred the overwrought Victorian-era rockeries that put rocks first and plants second. He believed that rock gardens should be constructed to provide the best advantage for alpine plants, take their cues from nature, use local stone if possible, and be built in sites "as graceful, quiet, and natural as they can be made."[18] English plant explorer Reginald Farrer (1880–1920) fueled the growing craze for rock gardens with two books: *My Rock Garden* (1907) and the two-volume *The English Rock Garden* (1919), still considered the authoritative work on the subject. Farrer echoed Robinson's derision for inelegant, unnatural rockeries, describing them as "almond puddings of spikes" or "dog's graves."[19] He was steadfastly opposed to the use of artificial stone and wrote "far better a rock garden without a single rock than ill-furnished acres of Portland cement blocks or sham stalactites."[20]

T. H. Everett's genius for rock placement is evident in this 1934 image of the Rock Garden after the first phase of construction was completed. MERTZ LIBRARY, NYBG.

Everett deeply admired Farrer and described *The English Rock Garden* as the "bible of rock gardeners everywhere."[21] Farrer's influence was clear in a series of articles Everett published in the *Gardener's Chronicle* in 1933 and 1934 as he was directing construction of the Rock Garden at NYBG. Like Robinson and Farrer, Everett viewed rock gardens first and foremost as environments for growing plants unsuited to cultivation in more traditional garden settings. However, Everett recognized that many of the true alpines featured in British and European rock gardens could not survive in New York's humid summer climate. At NYBG he ultimately created a garden of plants that grow harmoniously with rocks rather than a true alpine garden.

Everett had a very strong vision for the way rocks should be laid to provide both the best environments for plants and the most natural and beautiful effect. He distinguished between "natural" rock gardens, which incorporated existing rock, and "artificial" rock gardens, built entirely with imported rock. Everett looked to nature for inspiration. "To be convincing," he wrote, "the effect must be that [the rocks] were positioned by nature without aid from man. Here, if ever, true art is to conceal art."[22]

The location Everett chose, which he described as "a beautiful natural setting with a splendid background of forest,"[23] provided the ideal canvas for true rock gardening art. It is nestled into a gently sloping, south-facing valley adjacent to the northwestern edge of the Forest. The site was mostly open prior to construction, although there were some ancient native shade trees that were preserved and remain today. Glacially sculpted rock outcrops on the eastern and western borders of the site created an appropriate setting for building a "natural" rock garden. The abundance of weathered natural stones across the landscape provided ample raw materials for rock work that, with the right eye, could be arranged to appear as if positioned by nature.

Everett's genius for rock placement is evident. Photographs of the construction show how he and a team of gardeners moved and set hundreds of large rocks using horses, levers, chain hoists, and brute force. For the bulk of the garden, Everett chose rocks that were much longer than high, laid them end to end, and buried them to create the illusion of bedrock ridges poking through the soil surface. The general grain of the rock work dips gently from the edges of the site toward a stream that gurgles through the middle of

Cinnamon fern fiddleheads add texture along the Rock Garden stream.

NYBG horticulturists moved and placed vast quantities of rocks during the construction of the Rock Garden without the benefit of modern hydraulic equipment.
MERTZ LIBRARY, NYBG.

the garden. Everett carefully positioned rocks to form a cascade that seems to emerge from just above the natural ledge that defines the eastern edge of the site, furthering the illusion that the garden's rocks and watercourses have been formed by geological rather than horticultural forces. The garden also includes a small "alpine meadow" that provides a place for the eye to rest and a pond, added a few years after the initial phase of construction.

For Everett, as for Robinson and Farrer, the raison d'être for the constructed elements of a rock garden is to support rich and varied plantings. While edelweiss, draba (*Draba* spp.), alpine primrose (*Primula alpina*), and many of the other traditional alpine flowers that grace British and European rock gardens cannot survive the Bronx's summer heat and humidity, Everett set out to make the Rock Garden the most intensively planted and diverse garden at NYBG. He experimented with thousands of different plants over nearly forty years to create layers of color, texture, and form that blend harmoniously with the natural setting and provide sophisticated beauty in all seasons.

The floral display in the Rock Garden begins as early as mid-February when the charming lavender flowers of hardy cyclamen (*Cyclamen coum*) open above mottled green-and-white foliage. A rapid succession of early bulbs—snowdrop (*Galanthus* spp.), winter aconite (*Eranthis hyemalis*), crocus (*Crocus* spp.), reticulate iris (*Iris reticulata*), glory-of-

Above: *Iris reticulata* 'Katherine Hodgkin'.
MARLON CO, NYBG.
Opposite: Flowering dogwoods and a magnificent white oak at the edge of the Rock Garden pond.
Overleaf: Irises grow in a variety of habitats across the Rock Garden.
MARLON CO, NYBG.

Above: *Iris* 'Pauline' emerges
from the foliage of cyclamen.
MARLON CO, NYBG.
Right: Primroses and ferns line
the cascade stream that runs
through the middle of the Rock
Garden.

the-snow (*Chionodoxa forbesii*), squill (*Scilla* spp.), to name a few—come into flower as winter transitions into spring. Color continues to build in the garden from April, when candy tuft (*Iberis sempervirens*), fairy foxglove (*Erinus alpinus*), rockcress (*Arabis* spp.), basket-of-gold (*Aurinia saxatalis*), and other early perennials open, and reaches its peak in May, when the mats of mossy phlox (*Phlox subulata*) illuminate nearly every area of the garden and the improbable pouch-like flowers of lady's slipper orchids (*Cypripedium* spp.) and irises (*Iris* spp.) in all the colors of the rainbow open above the gathering green of later season alpines and perennials. Larger, fuller perennials such as bellflower, foxglove (*Digitalis* spp.), and salvia (*Salvia* spp.) thrive in the longer, hotter days of June. The garden quiets a bit in the summer, but it lights up again in fall when the towering oaks, sweet gums, and other native trees Everett preserved reach their full autumn glory. In winter, the sculptural forms of dwarf conifers echo the sophisticated beauty of Everett's rock work.

The Rock Garden has undergone several restorations since its completion. The goal of each of these projects has been to preserve its timeless beauty while repairing the elaborate infrastructure that underlies that beauty. In recent years, we have focused on making the Rock Garden more sustainable and resilient. In Everett's time, the cascade, stream, and pond were fed by an open tap. In 2014 we installed a recirculating system and completed the reconstruction and relining of the cascade, stream, and pond to minimize water loss.

Above: Pollinators and people appreciate the summer flowers of rusty foxglove.
MARLON CO, NYBG.
Opposite: T. H. Everett carefully placed the rocks on the cascade to create a series of dynamic falls and shallow pools.

We have been rejuvenating or replacing overgrown shrubs and small trees that threaten to undermine the garden's carefully composed scale. Curator Michael Hagen combed the NYBG archives to better understand Everett's design intent and is working with the Horticulture team to lift and reset portions of the original rockwork that have settled over time. Hagen has also maintained Everett's spirit of experimentation by sourcing, propagating, and planting new bulbs, perennials, shrubs, and small trees likely to thrive in the changing climate.

Above: Troughs at the entrance to the Rock Garden allow for the display of alpine plants not well suited to our soils and climate.
Right: The cascade in autumn.
Overleaf: Everett's siting of the Rock Garden seems particularly well considered in fall.

Daffodil Valley

IN 1982 NYBG HORTICULTURISTS ESTABLISHED A NEW DAFFODIL DISPLAY in a shaded valley adjacent to the Forest northwest of the Rock Garden. This new collection was inspired by the great success of Daffodil Hill, which had continued to provide a reliably uplifting display of flowers year after year with very little care. The creation of the new display was supported by a gift from the family of Murray Liasson, who grew up in the Bronx and fondly remembered his annual visits to Daffodil Hill with his mother. The daffodil collection in Daffodil Valley was Daffodil Hill with a twist.

The twist was that instead of mixed masses of relatively few types of daffodils, former NYBG horticulturists Michael Ruggiero and Greg Piotrowski organized Daffodil Valley as a display of all thirteen horticultural divisions of the genus *Narcissus* as classified by the Royal Horticultural Society. This classification is based on the number and shape of the flowers, which are divided into three sections: the tube at the base of the flower where it joins the scape, an outer ring of six petal-like tepals, and central corona, which is typically cylindrical but can take different forms. In the initial planting, cultivars from each division were planted near each other to form masses of similar plants. This arrangement echoed Britton and Brinley's original design for NYBG's living collections: related plants

Narcissus 'Early Bride', a large-cupped daffodil that flowers in mid-April. MARLON CO, NYBG.

Daffodil Valley typically finishes
flowering by early May as the
azaleas are reaching peak.

arranged in sequence across the landscape so that students could observe their similarities and differences.

The conditions in Daffodil Valley are very different from those on Daffodil Hill. The area is shaded by mature trees, including oak, tulip tree, sweetgum, and tupelo (*Nyssa sylvatica*). The valley captures rainwater from the surrounding slopes and becomes quite wet—bordering on sodden—in winter and early spring. Over time, the combination of shade and wet soil winnowed out many of the daffodil cultivars planted in the early 1980s. By the early 2000s, the original sequence of plantings had been interrupted beyond the point of recognition or repair. In response to these challenges, we have rethought the initial goal of displaying representatives of all horticultural divisions of *Narcissus* in sequence. We now source daffodils we think might be adapted to the moist shade and plant them where we think they are most likely to thrive rather than where they would have fallen in the original sequence. Even with this altered approach, eleven of the horticultural divisions are represented in Daffodil Valley—only the *bulbocodium*-type and *other daffodil cultivar*-type are absent.

Narcissus 'February Gold' is a *cyclamineus*-type daffodil that opens in March.
MARLON CO, NYBG.

Daffodil Valley begins flowering slightly later than Daffodil Hill, reflecting the difference in climate between the two locations. The first daffodil to flower is typically 'February Gold', a brilliant-yellow *cyclamineus*-type that usually opens in late March but has been in full

Narcissus 'Beersheba' is a trumpet-type daffodil with a white perianth and white corona. MARLON CO, NYBG.

flower as early as mid-February during particularly warm winters. Highlights of early April include 'Bravoure', a *trumpet*-type with large white tepals and a bright yellow corona, 'Birma', a *small-cupped*-type with yellow tepals and an orange corona, and 'Cassatta', a *split-corona*-type with greenish-white tepals and a greenish-yellow corona frilled and divided at the tips. Dozens of cultivars flower at the peak of the season in mid-to-late April. While *large-cupped*-types such as 'Pink Charm', with white tepals and a white corona tipped with a coral ring, predominate, *jonquilla*-types including bright yellow 'Sweetness', *double*-types including white and yellow 'Madison', *tazetta*-types including the white and orange 'Geranium', and *triandrus*-types including pure-white 'Rippling Waters' can also be enjoyed in Daffodil Valley during peak bloom. 'Dactyl', 'Cantabile', and other *poeticus*-types, fragrant with white tepals and very small disc-shaped coronas, are the last to flower, often remaining open into May.

The shade cast by the trees in Daffodil Valley is challenging for some daffodils, but the trees themselves create a lovely environment that is quite different from the wide-open expanse of Daffodil Hill. Their foliage emerges as the daffodils come into bloom, creating a filtered, soft green light that complements the masses of yellow and white on the ground plane. Smaller trees, including several varieties of flowering cherry, flowering dogwood (*Cornus florida*), and kousa dogwood (*Cornus kousa*), add a layer of nuanced charm. Daffodil Valley's cool shade provides welcome respite when spring's daffodils have given way to the diaphanous flower heads of unmown summer grass. At around the time new daffodils are planted in November, the valley feels like a continuation of the electric autumn color of the adjacent Forest.

It takes little focused effort to keep Daffodil Valley engaging and beautiful. Just as on Daffodil Hill, we cut the grass after the bulb foliage has died back—usually around the first week of July. We plant some new daffodils every fall, either to trial new cultivars or replace old favorites that have withered away. We will continue to search for varieties that will allow us to feature all thirteen divisions in Daffodil Valley as per the original concept, but we will not worry too much if we are not successful. After all, the essence of nature-sensitive gardening is to observe, adjust, and enjoy.

Due to its shady, protected spot, Daffodil Valley tends to reach peak bloom a week or so after Daffodil Hill, extending the daffodil season for Garden visitors.

Mature oaks, sweetgums,
tupelos, and other shade trees
extend the Daffodil Valley's
horticultural appeal into all four
seasons.

Maureen K. Chilton
Azalea Garden

THE INTRICATE DETAIL of the Rock Garden's constructed features and diverse plantings shows how careful observation of nature can inform and elevate horticulture. The breathtaking scale of the Maureen K. Chilton Azalea Garden reveals how gardening with nature can uplift and transport us. Completed in 2011, the Azalea Garden embodies NYBG's commitment to combining the artistry and drama of traditional ornamental horticulture with nature-sensitive design.

Spread across approximately eight acres between the Thain Family Forest and Daffodil Hill, the Azalea Garden takes full advantage of the mature trees, exposed rock outcrops, and dramatic topography that characterize the NYBG site. Like the Rock Garden, the Azalea Garden supports NYBG's mission as a botanical garden by featuring a diversity of woody and herbaceous plants from North America, Europe, and temperate Asia. Mature tulip tree, oaks, sweetgum, elms, maples, and other native shade trees that predate NYBG's presence provide high shade that creates optimal growing conditions for thousands of azalea and rhododendron (*Rhododendron* spp.) planted across the site's ridges, slopes, and depressions. Dogwood (*Cornus* spp.), magnolia (*Magnolia* spp.), redbud (*Cercis canadensis*), and other small flowering trees soften the transition between the trunks of the soaring canopy trees and the densely planted ground plane. The varied

This prominent rock outcrop was quarried for the construction of buildings during the Lorillard era.

foliage and flowers of companion shrubs add texture and extend the flowering season. Elegant sweeps of herbaceous plants finish the composition.

Azaleas, and the closely related rhododendrons, headline the Azalea Garden for good reason. They are ideal for nature-inspired gardening in New York's climate. They thrive in the acid soils that predominate in our woodlands, grow well in the shade of deciduous trees, combine nicely with a broad range of shade-tolerant perennials, and require little specialized care. There are dozens of hardy species, including many natives, and hundreds of cultivated varieties, which flower freely and generously in hues ranging from soft pastels to blazing oranges. Most are relatively slow growing and compact; larger, faster-growing species respond well to thoughtful pruning.

Prior to the development of the Chilton Azalea Garden, several azalea and rhododendron collections came and went in various settings within the landscape over the decades. In 1940 rhododendron breeder Charles O. Dexter donated a collection of rhododendron hybrids, which the Horticulture staff planted along the northern edge of the Forest in what is now Daffodil Valley. In the early 1940s, NYBG staff planted hundreds of azaleas along an ephemeral stream in a wooded valley in the southwestern corner of the Garden between the conifer plantations and the Bronx River. In 1969 the Garden established an azalea collection on a wooded slope between Daffodil Hill and the western boundary of the Forest in honor of long-serving trustee Sherman Baldwin.

In the mid-1980s, NYBG staff and students from the School of Professional Horticulture, a professional training program established by T. H. Everett in the 1930s, transplanted approximately five hundred azaleas and rhododendrons from Target Rock, the former

The high tree canopy of the Azalea Garden creates the perfect environment for shade-loving herbaceous plants such as hosta, hellebores, and Hakone-grass.

The Azalea Garden's paths
and plantings were designed
in response to the site's
remarkable natural rocks and
venerable trees.

estate of financier Ferdinand Eberstadt on the North Shore of Long Island, to various places across the Garden, including the site of the Baldwin collection. This site is ideal for growing azaleas. Dozens of mature native shade trees preserved since NYBG's founding, some more than 150 feet tall, form a high canopy that creates the bright shade that azaleas require to thrive. The woodland soil is acidic and rich in organic material. Massive glacially sculpted rock outcrops create dramatic topography with more than 60 feet of elevation change across the site. A seep and an ephemeral stream in the south end provide suitable habitat for moisture-loving plants.

The Eberstadt collection included a mix of named cultivars and unnamed seedlings developed by Eberstadt himself. NYBG staff planted the azaleas, mostly evergreen and semi-evergreen hybrids of Asian species with flowers in the cool range of the spectrum, in masses across the broad, south-facing slope in the center of the site and along the edges of the pre-existing path network developed soon after the Garden's 1915 expansion. Flowering for a brief but intense period in early May, these azaleas quickly became a highlight of NYBG's spring season.

As beautiful as the azalea collection was, its pathways and plantings had some shortcomings. The historic paths cut across the topography awkwardly and were extremely steep in sections, making them difficult to navigate for many visitors. There were no gathering areas or vistas where visitors could stop and take in the dramatic views of the azaleas and surrounding landscape. The azaleas, which represented a relatively narrow range of cultivars, flowered over a short period of time and did not fully showcase the beauty and adaptability

Hosta 'First Frost' thrives in the Azalea Garden.

of this fantastic garden plant. There were no companion plantings to extend the flowering season or break up the monotonous texture of the azalea foliage after the flowers had faded. Once the flowering finished, there was little to draw visitors in to explore the natural beauty of the site.

In 2007 we worked with landscape architect Laurie Olin and his firm to develop a master plan to revitalize the "Heart of the Garden," a group of connected landscapes, including the Forest, Native Plant Garden, Rock Garden, and the Azalea Garden. The Olin plan proposed a design vocabulary that would visually connect each of these related but programmatically distinct landscapes. Like the *General Plan* and the Olmsted Brothers report, the Olin plan acknowledged the picturesque beauty of the site's natural features and suggested ways to incorporate that natural beauty into the designed landscapes. It also provided guidelines for the sorts of materials that should be used to construct paths, walls, and other built elements so that they, too, fit elegantly within the larger landscape.

The timing of the Olin plan was fortuitous. In 2008 we began working with Shavaun Towers of Towers|Golde and Sheila Brady of Oehme, van Sweden to help us transform the azalea collection into the Azalea Garden. Our goals for this new feature were to celebrate (and preserve) the site's varied topography, exposed rock outcrops, and venerable native trees—all while improving access, creating gathering areas with vistas across the landscape, planting thousands of azaleas and rhododendrons, and extending the season of interest by incorporating companion shrubs, flowering trees, and herbaceous plants. This new garden would be built on the first principle of nature-friendly gardening—adapt your plan to the site rather than the site to your plan.

The bright yellow fall foliage of Arkansas blue star lights up the understory of the Azalea Garden and complements the color of the site's many shade trees.

Every available pocket in the
Azalea Garden, including
seams of shallow soil within and
adjacent to rock outcrops and
ledges, has been planted.

We envisioned a layered garden that would be breathtaking in early May, when the bulk of the azaleas flower, and remain horticulturally captivating when the azaleas were not in bloom. Former curator Jessica Schuler sourced more than 3,500 azaleas and rhododendrons for the expanded collection. To ensure that these new plants would fit well with the existing collection, she noted the bloom times and colors of the azaleas that remained from earlier plantings and hunted for varieties that would blend well with those established plants. Schuler identified an impressive selection of new azaleas and rhododendrons, ranging from Korean rhododendron (*Rhododendron mucronulatum*), which flowers in March, to Encore® azaleas, which flower in November. She also added many North American species azaleas, including swamp azalea (*Rhododendron viscosum*), early azalea (*Rhododendron prinophyllum*), smooth azalea (*Rhododendron arborescens*), pinxterbloom azalea (*Rhododendron pericylmenoides*), and plumleaf azalea (*Rhododendron prunifolium*) to add subtle beauty and support native pollinators.

While the Azalea Garden derives much of its complex beauty from azaleas and rhododendrons, its name does not fully capture the diversity and layered sophistication of its plantings. To stretch out the flowering season and add a variety of plant forms and foliage textures, we added hundreds of flowering shrubs, including native and Asian witch-hazel (*Hamamelis* spp.), various hydrangea (*Hydrangea* spp.) and hydrangea relatives, Virginia sweetspire (*Itea virginiana*), bottlebrush buckeye (*Aesculus parviflora*), and many more. Collectively, the Azalea Garden's trees and shrubs provide flowers from early March well into December. They also combine to create one of the most magical autumn displays at NYBG.

The lavender-pink flowers of Rhododendron 'Karen', a hybrid azalea, add welcome color to the entrance.

Peak azalea season occurs
in the first two weeks of May.
This part of the garden is called
"Mother's Day Slope" because
it is often in full flower on the
second Sunday in May.

The Azalea Garden's trees and shrubs form the backbone of the garden but are only partly responsible for its appeal. Margaret Falk, then Associate Vice President for Horticulture, and Kristin Schleiter worked with the Oehme, van Sweden team to create an ambitious herbaceous planting plan appropriate to the scale of the site. Taking advantage of the range of soil types, aspects, and exposures found across the garden, they assembled an impressive plant list that included everything from winter-flowering snowdrop to fall-flowering Japanese anemone (*Anemone japonica*). Including such a broad range of plants allowed us to make the Azalea Garden a botanical garden unto itself, with carefully curated collections of some of our favorite woodland perennials, bulbs, ferns, and sedges.

We created a "summit meadow" inspired by Appalachian "balds" at the highest point of the garden, which is a welcome sunny patch within the mostly shaded site. Here a seasonal progression of bulbs and perennials emerges from a matrix of grasses and sedges in early spring to late fall. We incorporated more than one hundred varieties of hosta (*Hosta* spp.) throughout the garden, concentrating them along path edges so that visitors can get a close look at the bold, patterned leaves for which this genus is celebrated. We similarly took advantage of the opportunity to build our collection of barrenwort (*Epimedium* spp.) species and cultivars, favorites of contemporary gardeners for their deer resistance and tolerance of dry shade. We worked with snowdrop experts to build our collection of this winter-flowering gem. All told, we planted more than 70,000 perennials, ferns, grasses, and bulbs in the Azalea Garden before the garden opened and have continued to refine and enhance these plantings since 2011.

Fall-flowering Japanese anemone is an eye-catching companion to our native shade trees.

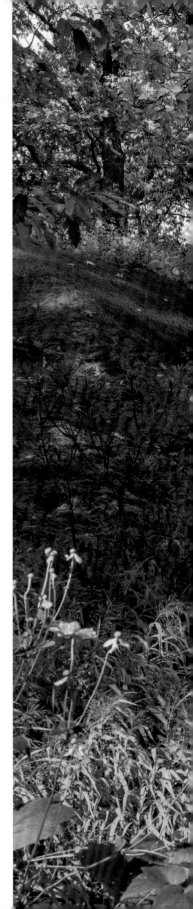

Opposite: This young Chinese cork oak will ultimately shade the next generation of azaleas and woodland perennials. Above: From this perspective, the Azalea Garden looks more like a simple woodland than the complex and layered garden it is.

If do no harm is the first principle of nature-friendly gardening, the second might be "right plant, right place." By taking the time to understand a site and selecting plants adapted to its specific conditions, a thoughtful gardener can minimize horticultural inputs while maximizing horticultural rewards. The Azalea Garden demonstrates this principle on a grand scale. Its carefully considered blend of native and introduced—but not invasive—garden plants, each placed where it has the best chance to thrive, creates layers of beauty that unfold with seasons. What more can we ask of a garden?

Above: An ephemeral stream at the south end of the garden.
Opposite: The foamy flowers of Astilbe 'Flamingo'.

A varied site and a commitment to the principle of "right plant, right place" supported the inclusion of an extraordinary diversity of plants in the Azalea Garden.

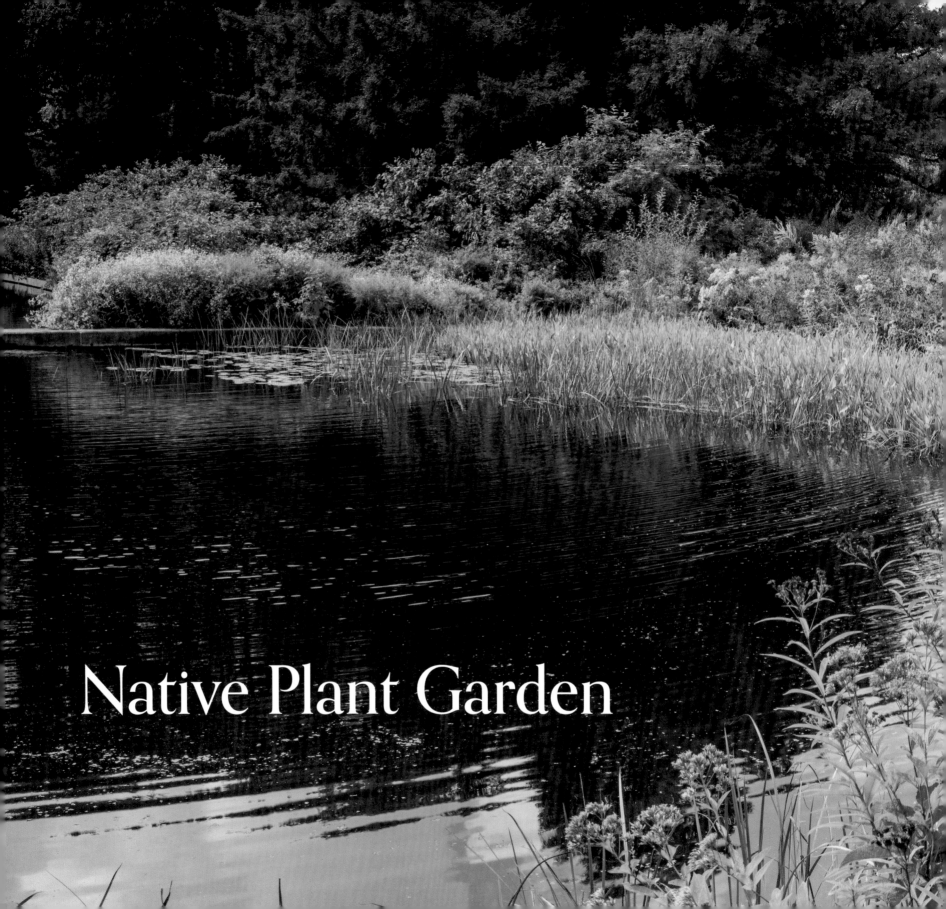

Native Plant Garden

THE SIMPLEST WAY TO GARDEN WITH NATURE is to add regionally native plants to your garden. Well-chosen native plants will enhance the beauty of gardens of any size or style and provide immediate benefits to local birds, bees, butterflies, and other wildlife. Native plants connect a garden to its larger ecological context and make it a functioning part of its place.

Interest in gardening with native plants in America has ebbed and flowed since the mid-nineteenth century. In *A Treatise on the Theory and Practice of Landscape Gardening* (1844), Alexander Jackson Downing (1815–1852) extols the virtues of native American trees, but he does not go so far as to call for the exclusive or extensive use of native plants in American landscapes. Similarly, Frederick Law Olmsted acknowledged the virtues of native trees, but he also used many introduced species in the large parks and campuses he designed. Beatrix Farrand, Ellen Shipman, and Marian Coffin—the most respected and prolific garden designers of the first half of the twentieth century—incorporated native trees, shrubs, and wildflowers into their designs, but again did not advocate for their sole use.

Little bluestem and flowering spurge in the dry meadow of the Native Plant Garden.

Jens Jensen (1860–1951), who emigrated from Denmark to America in 1884 and worked his way up from park laborer to superintendent of Chicago's West Park System, was a pioneer in the use of native plants in parks and gardens. His first experiment was the creation of an American Garden in Union Park, a small park on the west side of Chicago, which he filled with wildflowers transplanted from the park's wild areas. These plants performed much better in the temperamental climate and heavy clay soils than the exotic plants commonly used at the time. Inspired by this success and concerned about the rapid loss of natural areas throughout the Midwest, Jensen became a strong advocate for nature-inspired design over a long career, developing both public landscapes and private gardens from Michigan to Maine.

Jensen was largely motivated by the aesthetic and practical benefits of using native plants in designed landscapes. Some of his contemporaries saw gardening with native plants as a way to educate gardeners and convert them into conservationists. Broad interest in native plant gardens was inspired in part by the decline of wildflower populations in the early twentieth century, particularly in natural areas in and near cities. In 1902, concerned about the indiscriminate harvest of wildflowers in NYBG's Forest and other New York parks, Elizabeth Britton co-founded the Wildflower Preservation Society of America, a plant conservation organization modeled after the Audubon Society. Similarly concerned by the rapid decline of wildflowers in Minnesota, in 1907 botanist and educator Eloise Butler (1851–1933) helped create the Wild Botanical Garden, America's first public garden dedicated solely to native plants, in Glenwood Park in Minneapolis.

Bryologist, conservationist, and NYBG co-founder Elizabeth Britton studying plants in 1890.
MERTZ LIBRARY, NYBG.

Elizabeth Britton spent decades extolling the virtues of native plants and rallying the public in their support. She wrote more than thirty essays on the subject, including fourteen in a series titled "Wild Plants Needing Our Protection" published in the *Journal of The New York Botanical Garden*. After her death in 1934, NYBG staff began developing an informal wildflower garden in her memory in a glade south of the Rock Garden. This small garden was officially dedicated on May 9, 1940, by the New York Bird and Tree Club. In 1958 the NYBG Native Plant Garden Committee formed to solicit support for and guide the expansion of this modest native plant garden. Over the next several decades, the garden grew and ultimately became a sort of living diorama with displays based on regional ecosystems, including Hempstead Plains on Long Island and the Pine Barrens in New Jersey, and plant habitats with specialized soil types, including a serpentine barren and a limestone cobble.

NYBG's original native plant garden was dedicated to Britton, who made many contributions to botanical science and plant conservation. MERTZ LIBRARY, NYBG.

This artificial approach to recreating complex ecosystems on a small scale ultimately failed horticulturally and aesthetically. By the early 2000s, the garden lacked visual cohesion and became challenging to maintain. Fortunately, NYBG trustee Shelby White saw the potential for the garden, and, with her support, in 2008 we retained Oehme, van Sweden to help us to completely remake it. From the beginning of this collaboration, we kept the core principles of nature-informed gardening in mind. Instead of depending on artificial

Opposite: Bee balm in flower
along the edge of the Native
Plant Garden pool.
Above: A cultivar of narrowleaf
ironweed in flower near the
entrance.

re-creations of natural habitats to support a diversity of native plants, we looked closely at the 3.5-acre site's natural mix of soil, hydrology, shade, and slope and chose plants that would thrive in those conditions. Our goal was to showcase as many, or more, native plant species as had been grown in the original native plant garden, but to do so in a way that would reflect the site's natural qualities rather than erase them.

The garden has a central valley bordered by two rocky ridges aligned along a north-south axis. The eastern ridge, which borders the Thain Family Forest, is shaded by mature native trees, including some that predate NYBG's establishment and others that were part of the original native plant garden. The valley and the western ridge are largely open, with a few mature oaks and a pair of Japanese nutmeg-yews (*Torreya nucifera*). The central valley slopes gently to the south and drains into a nearby wetland that ultimately connects to the Bronx River. The soils across the site are generally well-drained acidic sandy loams.

Former curators Jody Payne and Deanna Curtis worked with Sheila Brady and her team at Oehme, van Sweden to develop a planting plan that takes advantage of the site's lovely mix of sun and shade and wet and dry. We chose woodland shrubs, wildflowers, and ferns for the shaded east side of the garden. The center of the garden was transformed into a water feature that consists of three connected pools, the uppermost of which features aquatic plants and a small bog. The sunbaked western slope provided the ideal conditions for meadow grasses and forbs. The topography creates a distinct moisture gradient within each section of the garden, allowing us to showcase a range of drought-tolerant and moisture-loving plants within a relatively small area.

Yellow coneflowers appear to float above the lacy flowers of tufted hairgrass in the mesic meadow.

Oehme, van Sweden is known for using large masses of plants to create striking displays across large areas. While the Native Plant Garden does include massed plantings appropriate to the scale of the site, NYBG's desire to feature the greatest possible diversity of regionally native plants inspired a more nuanced design approach. In the woodland sections of the garden, clusters of trillium (*Trillium* spp.), bloodroot (*Sanguinaria canadensis*), and other spring ephemeral wildflowers grow within a loose matrix of ferns, sedges, and other shade-tolerant herbaceous plants that shade the soil in the heat of the summer when the ephemerals are dormant. In the meadow, little bluestem (*Schizachyrium scoparium*), lovegrass (*Eragrostis* spp.), and other grasses provide structure, while waves of bee balm (*Monarda* spp.), coneflower (*Echinacea* spp.), goldenrods (*Solidago* spp.), and aster (various genera) create bursts of seasonal color. The whole garden comes alive in fall as the brilliant foliage of maple, tupelo, oak, hickory, and other shade trees complements the tawny tones of the senescent ferns, grasses, and forbs.

The primary goal of the Native Plant Garden is to celebrate the diversity and beauty of our region's flora. It was also designed to draw visitors in and encourage them to linger long enough to develop a fondness for native plants. Brady and her team used modern and sustainable materials and construction techniques to create accessible paths, places to sit and reflect, and outdoor classrooms. The paths, constructed from permeable, resin-stabilized gravel, were laid out to avoid damaging the mature native trees in the woodlands and to highlight the site's geological features, including glacially sculpted rock outcrops and a large glacial erratic boulder known as "Split Rock." To compensate for water lost to evaporation, the pools recycle stormwater collected beneath the permeable

The paths of the Native Plant Garden were designed to give visitors the opportunity to get up close to "Split Rock," a boulder of Yonkers Gneiss deposited by a glacier nearly 20,000 years ago.

Opposite: Smooth aster is
one of many aster species
that flower in the Native Plant
Garden meadow in autumn.
Above: Flowering dogwood and
ostrich fern are planted in the
moist woodland along the edge
of the central pool.

paths and stored in a 50,000-gallon underground cistern. An accessible boardwalk along the edge of the pools is made of kiln-dried black locust (*Robinia pseudoacacia*), a tree native to the Southeast and Midwest that has become naturalized in New York. The stone walls and weirs are dark Hamilton sandstone quarried in the Catskills.

Since its opening in 2013, the Native Plant Garden has been extraordinarily popular among visitors, both human and nonhuman. It is the best location at NYBG to observe butterflies, starting with the earliest mourning cloaks to autumn's last monarchs. In the summer, bats and swallows hunt for insects in the evening skies while damselflies and dragonflies flit over the frog-filled pools. In winter, juncos and white-throated sparrows pick seeds from the dried flower spikes of dormant meadow plants while red-tailed hawks circle above hoping to catch one of the many mice and chipmunks that scurry beneath the tangled mat of stalks. The Native Plant Garden proves that gardening with nature benefits all living things.

A fresh layer of snow reveals the "bones" of the Native Plant Garden, which nestles into a gently sloping valley.

Opposite: The Native Plant
Garden blends elegantly with the
adjacent Thain Family Forest.
Above: A grand red oak creates
a shady nook above the pool.

The way the plants respond to
the ever-changing quality of
light across the seasons makes
each visit to the Native Plant
Garden feel like a completely
new experience.

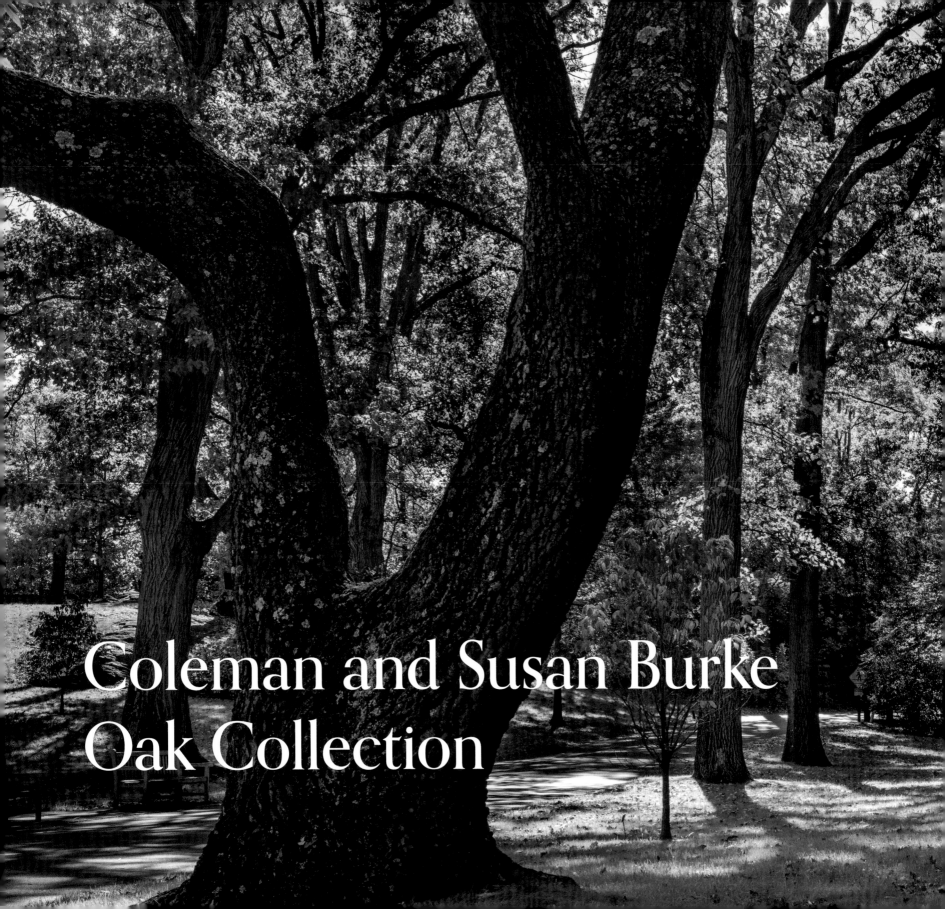

Coleman and Susan Burke
Oak Collection

BRITTON AND BRINLEY'S *General Plan* allocated about 100 acres for tree collections that would serve NYBG's research and education mission. Thirty acres were reserved for a pinetum—pines, spruces, and other conifers—and 70 acres were dedicated to a deciduous arboretum—maples, elms, oaks, and other non-coniferous trees. At the time of NYBG's founding, the landscape outside the Forest was already effectively a deciduous arboretum, with hundreds of mature native trees growing in the pastures that surrounded the Forest. These native trees were considered NYBG's first living plant collection and figured prominently in the design of the landscape. In 1897 Britton wrote:

> In planning the positions of roads, paths, and planted areas, careful attention
> has been given to the preservation of all the perfect and healthy standing
> trees possible. The areas to be treated as forest will be subsequently
> described. In the systematic planting of the pinetum, the deciduous
> arboretum, and the decorative grounds, these specimen trees have been
> kept, even if they come into positions not demanded by the arrangement
> adopted. The arrangement of the deciduous arboretum has been so adapted
> that in many cases they come into place.[24]

Male oak flowers are held in catkins that hang below the emerging leaves in spring.

Britton and Brinley laid out the Deciduous Arboretum on the east side of the Bronx River, with the oak collection in a prominent location on a rocky plateau overlooking the river. In 1898 NYBG horticulturists began planting oaks from Asia, Europe, and other parts of the United States to augment the seven species native to our site: white oak (*Quercus alba*), chestnut oak (*Quercus montana*), swamp white oak (*Quercus bicolor*), pin oak (*Quercus palustris*), scarlet oak (*Quercus coccinea*), red oak (*Quercus rubra*), and black oak (*Quercus velutina*). By 1917 the collection comprised thirty-five different oak species and cultivated varieties. While most of the original Deciduous Arboretum was lost to the expansion of the Bronx River Parkway in 1937, the oak collection was spared. Today it features some

of the oldest planted trees at NYBG, including swamp white oak grown from acorns that Nathaniel Britton collected on Staten Island in 1896.

Above: The leaves of shingle oak are unlobed and look nothing like the oaks of most people's imaginations. Opposite: This seating wall is made from stone quarried in the Catskills that blends beautifully with the site's bedrock.

Between 2020 and 2022, we updated and enhanced the historic oak collection with the support and encouragement of trustee Susan Burke in honor of her husband, Coleman, who loved oaks. We worked with Towers|Golde to create a network of accessible paths that lead to elegant seat walls—made with the same dark Hamilton sandstone used in the Native Plant Garden—with long views into the adjacent Forest and Magnolia Collection. We opened up growing space by pruning the mature oaks in the collection and clearing

Native smooth (left) and oakleaf
(right) hydrangea add summer
flowers to the Burke Oak
Collection.

invasive vines and shrubs from the rock outcrops that emerge across the site. We planted hybrid arborvitae (*Thuja* spp.) to screen the adjacent Bronx River Parkway and softened the transition to the adjacent woodlands with flowering dogwood and native shrubs, including oakleaf hydrangea *(Hydrangea quercifolia)* and smooth hydrangea *(Hydrangea arborescens)*. We used every available inch of sunny ground to add twenty-five new oaks to the collection, including several we had never grown before at NYBG.

Deanna Curtis sourced these new oaks from nurseries across the United States. She carefully selected a range of species and cultivated varieties that would showcase the diversity of size, habit, foliage, and even acorn shape within the genus. Highlights include Compton's oak (*Quercus* X *comptoniae*), a hybrid between live oak (*Quercus virginiana*) and overcup oak (*Quercus lyrata*); cut-leaf Daimyo oak (*Quercus dentata* 'Pinnatifida'), which has leaves so deeply divided they don't appear to have any leaf blades at all; and *Quercus baronii*, a semi-evergreen oak endemic to China. We planted these new young trees in openings in the nearly closed canopy created by the outstretched limbs of the dozens of mature oaks that remain from the initial plantings of the early 1900s.

Although not as floriferous or flashy as the other gardens and collections we have revitalized over the past few decades, the Burke Oak Collection has a quiet elegance that reveals itself to anyone fortunate to wander its paths and take a closer look. The massive trunks of the mature oaks frame views and lend an air of timelessness. The newly planted trees exude promise and invite close investigation. Their beauty is in their fine details: the dark hues of their emerging leaves, the intricate patterns created by the overlapping scales of their winter buds, the way their new shoots extend toward openings in the canopy above.

Opposite: The translucent
emerging foliage of oaks glows
soft green in the spring light.
Above: The new leaves of
Quercus baronii, a semi-
evergreen oak native to China,
have a bronze cast.

Oaks are unmatched among shade trees for their beauty, diversity, and longevity, which should be reason enough to plant one. They are also ideal for nature-inspired gardening because of their extraordinary ecological value. Wherever they grow, oaks support a bewildering diversity of insects, birds, and mammals. In his 2021 book *The Nature of Oaks*, entomologist Douglas Tallamy enumerates the many virtues of oaks and advocates for including them in our gardens. "If you are at all interested in contributing to the conservation of local animals, or in enjoying the wonders of nature right at home," he writes, "planting one or more oaks is an awfully good way to do those things."[25] If a single oak can transform a barren landscape into a nature-friendly garden, then imagine how the Burke Oak Collection, which includes more than 150 native and planted oaks, is benefiting nature in New York City.

A tulip tree, preserved since NYBG's founding, marks the transition from the Oak Collection to the adjacent Magnolia Collection.

Above: The coarsely toothed
leaves of *Quercus aliena*, native
to eastern Asia.
Right: Recently planted oaks are
the titans of the future.

Opposite: Oaks growing in the
shade of the adjacent Forest
tend to grow upright, with tall,
straight trunks reaching for
the light.
Above: The russet autumn leaves
of oaks mark the beginning of
the end of fall at NYBG.

Gardening into the Future

CITING NYBG AS A MODEL FOR NATURE-SENSITIVE GARDENING PRACTICES might seem unrealistic—absurd, perhaps—for the average American gardener. After all, most makers of public gardens or parks or campuses, let alone gardeners, lack the advantage of a "readymade" picturesque setting with an old-growth forest, a rushing river, exposed bedrock, and legions of ancient shade trees. It is true that the Brittons and the Scientific Directors gave NYBG a head start in their choice of our site. We strive to validate that choice every day as we enhance and care for the landscape and living collections in service of NYBG's mission.

NYBG's horticulturists do have some things in common with home gardeners when it comes to the day-to-day work required to keep the Garden healthy and beautiful. All gardens require planting, watering, weeding, fertilizing, composting, pruning, mowing, managing pests, and so on, whether the work is being done on a quarter-acre suburban plot or across 250 acres in the Bronx. The difference between them and us is a matter of training and scale, but the potential impacts of our horticultural practices on the natural environment are the same.

The Twin Lakes are currently being considered for a significant restoration project.

An enormous black oak, likely
more than two centuries old,
stands at the entrance to the
South Forest.

Opposite: The South Forest has great potential to be a showcase for nature-friendly gardening techniques.
Right: Horses helping gather the fuel they need to perform their work in 1917. MERTZ LIBRARY, NYBG.
Overleaf: The South Forest features some of NYBG's most noteworthy native trees.

NYBG is as much a museum of horticultural practices as it is a museum of plants. Our horticulturists have employed every new horticultural technique and used every new tool that has come along since 1895: scythes ultimately gave way to lawn mowers; horse-drawn wagons became pickup trucks; well-rotted manure was replaced by inorganic fertilizers; brass spigots evolved into computer-controlled irrigation heads; and so on. Each new tool or technique came with the promise of improved efficacy, safety, or efficiency.

Not all of these innovations lived up to their promise, and some have shown the potential to cause harm. Uncontrolled use of inorganic fertilizers can lead to algal blooms that choke ponds and lakes. The uninformed use of pesticides harms bees, butterflies, soil microbes, fish, and aquatic invertebrates. Excessive irrigation of non-climate-adapted garden plants, including lawns, wastes potable water and threatens aquifers. Some garden plants

hailed for their beauty and toughness have become invasive in natural areas where they outcompete and displace native species.

For the past twenty-five years, Associate Vice President for Horticulture Operations Kurt Morrell, who began his distinguished career at NYBG in the late 1980s as a student in our School of Professional Horticulture, has led the effort to assess our horticultural practices and refine them in support of our commitment to nature-sensitive gardening. We have developed a plant health program built on the principles of Integrated Pest Management to reduce our use of chemical pesticides and fertilizers. We

Above: Upper Twin Lake in 1901.
MERTZ LIBRARY, NYBG.
Opposite: South Forest has excellent access to the Bronx River.

created a Green Materials Recycling Center where we compost all of our organic waste so that we can reuse it to care for our plants. We have worked with nurseries around the world to source disease-resistant roses for the Peggy Rockefeller Rose Garden. We assess the potential invasiveness of plants before we consider adding them to our living collections. We are doing all of this to be better stewards of the environment and, we hope, to inspire people who look to us for inspiration to do the same.

A garden is never finished, and NYBG is no exception. We have restored or enhanced about 150 of the Garden's 250 acres since 2000. The remaining portions of the landscape have great potential for continuing our tradition of gardening with nature. Upcoming projects will include the Magnolia Collection, a historic tree collection adjacent to the

The historic Magnolia
Collection, established soon
after NYBG's founding, will soon
be expanded and enhanced
using the principles of nature-
friendly gardening.

Burke Oaks and the Thain Family Forest, the South Forest, nearly 20 acres of mixed forest along the west bank of the Bronx River at NYBG's southern end, and Twin Lakes, a 12-acre site on the northern border of the Garden that features a pair of small lakes surrounded by wetlands and woodlands. Each of the landscapes provides an opportunity to continue our tradition of gardening in harmony with nature. We will bring our growing ecological restoration and sustainable horticulture expertise to bear on the design, construction, and ongoing care of those sites. It is our hope that in another 130 years, home gardeners, landscape architects, and park-makers around the world will cite NYBG as their inspiration for creating green spaces that helped address the climate and biodiversity crises of the twenty-first century.

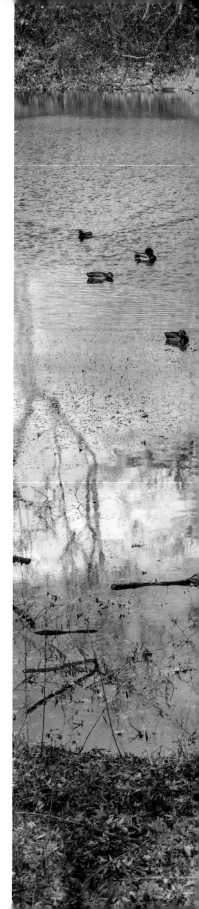

The Twin Lakes are havens for ducks, herons, egrets, and other waterfowl during the spring and fall migrations.

Right and overleaf: The South
Forest has all the characteristics
of an inspiring and engaging
outdoor classroom. Once its
restoration is complete, it will
be a place where students of all
ages can learn about how they
can help steward urban nature.

Notes

1   N. L. Britton, "Act of Incorporation," *Bulletin of The New York Botanical Garden* 1, no. 1 (April 15, 1896): 1–5.

2   N. L. Britton, "Report of the Secretary for 1895," *Bulletin of The New York Botanical Garden* 1, no. 1 (April 15, 1896): 13–14.

3   N. L. Britton, "The General Plan for The New York Botanical Garden," *Bulletin of The New York Botanical Garden* 1, no. 2 (January 1, 1897): 86.

4   Charles Sargent, "Natural Beauty in Urban Parks," *Garden and Forest* 10, no. 488 (June 30, 1897): 252.

5   N. L. Britton, "Report of the Secretary for 1895," *Bulletin of The New York Botanical Garden* 1, no. 1 (April 15, 1896): 17.

6   J. F. Kemp, "The Glacial or Post-Glacial Diversion of the Bronx River from Its Old Channel," *Bulletin of The New York Botanical Garden* 1, no. 2 (January 1, 1897): 78–85.

7   N. L. Britton, "Lists of Plants on the Grounds, 1898," *Bulletin of The New York Botanical Garden* 1, no. 4 (April 13, 1899): 195–203.

8   National Park Service National Register of Historic Places database (https://catalog.archives.gov/id/75315645).

9   Olmsted Brothers, *A Report on the New York Botanical Garden* (New York: 1924), 23.

10 Terryane E. Maenza-Gmelch, "Late-Glacial–Early Holocene Vegetation, Climate, and Fire at Sutherland Pond, Hudson Highlands, Southeastern New York, U.S.A.," *Canadian Journal of Botany* 75, no. 3 (March 1977): 431–39.

11 N. L. Britton, "The Hemlock Grove on the Banks of the Bronx River and What It Signifies," *Transactions of the Bronx Society of Arts and Sciences* 1, no. 1 (May 1906): 5.

12 N. L. Britton, "The Hemlock Grove on the Banks of the Bronx River and What It Signifies," *Transactions of the Bronx Society of Arts and Sciences* 1, no. 1 (May 1906): 7.

13 N. L. Britton, "The Hemlock Grove on the Banks of the Bronx River and What It Signifies," *Transactions of the Bronx Society of Arts and Sciences* 1, no. 1 (May 1906): 8.

14 Barrington Moore et al., "Hemlock and Its Environment," *Bulletin of The New York Botanical Garden* 12, no. 45 (September 13, 1924): 331.

15 Eliot Nagele et al., "A Century of Change in a Mature Urban Forest: The Thain Family Forest of the New York Botanical Garden, Bronx, New York," *Journal of Forestry*, 2024, fvad057, https://doi.org/10.1093/jofore/fvad057.

16 N. L. Britton, "Act of Incorporation," *Bulletin of The New York Botanical Garden* 1, no. 2 (January 1, 1897): 65.

17 Olmsted Brothers, *A Report on the New York Botanical Garden* (New York: 1924), 19.

18 William Robinson, *Alpine Flowers for English Gardens*, 2nd ed. (London: John Murray, 1875), 7.

19 Reginald Farrer, *The English Rock Garden*, vol 1. (London: T.C. & E.C. Mack, 1919), 40.

20 Reginald Farrer, *The English Rock Garden*, vol 1. (London: T.C. & E.C. Mack, 1919), 29.

21 T. H. Everett, *The New York Botanical Garden Encyclopedia of Horticulture,* vol. 9. (New York: Garland, 1982), 2945.

22 T. H. Everett, *The New York Botanical Garden Encyclopedia of Horticulture,* vol. 9. (New York: Garland, 1982), 2947.

23 T. H. Everett, "The Thompson Memorial Rock Garden," *Journal of The New York Botanical Garden* 33, no. 395 (November 1932): 256.

24 N. L. Britton et al., "Report of the Plans Commission," *Bulletin of The New York Botanical Garden* 1, no. 2 (January 1, 1897): 33.

25 Doug Tallamy, *The Nature of Oaks* (Portland, OR: Timber Press, 2021), 152.

The Cascade Slope in the Rock Garden is particularly beautiful in summer when bellflower, yarrow, and milkweeds are in flower.

Afterword

LARRY LEDERMAN

THIS IS THE END OF THE BOOK: TIME TO LOOK BACK AND REFLECT.

This is Todd Forrest's and my third book about the New York Botanical Garden. It is a departure from the others in that it is revelatory. The other two are descriptive, beautifully so, presenting what you see when you visit NYBG: exceptional flower beds, magnificent trees, and an extraordinary conservatory, symbolic of the garden.

This book reveals the landscape of NYBG, sylvan and craggy, formed by glaciers, through which the Bronx River flows and borders the Thain Family Forest, an uncut 50-acre forest of native trees. The Bronx River is barely visible in the most frequented areas of the garden, and the Forest is set apart, a place of its own. The tranquility within and the sense of the eternal is experienced on entry, and it is transportive. The Forest is the ultimate natural retreat in New York City.

A million daffodils burst forth in the spring and shine like the sun on Daffodil Hill. In Daffodil Valley, multiple varieties of daffodils flow like rivulets of water through the lawn, spreading a joyous spirit of vitality. The Maureen K. Chilton Azalea Garden is a natural Eden, a huge

A weeping Katsura tree at the entrance to Daffodil Valley.

area planted among glacial scarred rock and towering trees that shelter the azaleas and filter the light, enriching their colors. There is stunning diversity in the Native Plant Garden, which nurtures a flowering woodland and a brilliant meadow bordering the pond, expressive in every season. The Rock Garden is a work of art, an invitation to appreciate the divine in rocks and plantings. Mighty oaks and newly planted saplings grace the Coleman and Susan Burke Oak Collection. The great oaks engender wonder, and the saplings offer the comforting assurance of renewal.

Todd Forrest's text explains, and the photographs display, a multigenerational achievement. Each generation retunes its instruments to keep NYBG attuned to its heritage of sustainable gardening. Attention and devotion are required. Read carefully in the text about the work done and the choices made to keep the Forest a native haven. The Forest would seem to require little attention, but intrusion and change are inevitable.

Todd Forrest's horticultural stewardship has spanned more than twenty years, and much that is innovative and true to NYBG's gardening genius has been done on his watch. It has been my pleasure and delight to capture it in these photographs. It is our hope that these natural areas will receive ever-increasing appreciation and visitor attention and that future generations will look to this book as a resource as they, too, experience inevitable change in their gardening with nature.

These mature saucer magnolias, beloved by NYBG visitors, will be the centerpiece of the restored Magnolia Collection.

Acknowledgments

Jennifer Bernstein has supported this project ever since I introduced it to her very early in her tenure as CEO at NYBG. Her help in bringing the book to fruition is much appreciated.

Todd Forrest pointed the way and guided me on paths less traveled in the NYBG. His work is the inspiration for the book.

Elizabeth White and I have worked on six books together. She is a remarkable editor. Her fine hand and editorial acumen are fully reflected in this book, which I believe will significantly help it become a source of inspiration for many gardeners.

John Maggiotto is a master photographer and printer who has played an essential role in all my books and exhibitions. An outgrowth of our collaboration is our friendship, which I cherish.

My wife, Kitty Hawks, has helped to educate me in the arts. She has an extraordinary eye for beauty and is a consummate gardener. Her guidance is apparent here and in all that I have done.

I am grateful for all the help I have received from this group of friends and colleagues. I could not have done the book without them.

—LARRY LEDERMAN

It has been an extraordinary privilege to have spent nearly three decades working at the New York Botanical Garden, which is simultaneously steeped in noble tradition and committed to evolving in service of both people and the planet. I have been fortunate to work alongside scientists who are global experts in their fields, educators who cultivate the curiosity of everyone from Bronx kindergarteners to suburban retirees, and horticulturists who sow beauty and reap delight. Along the way, I have developed an awestruck appreciation for the foresight of NYBG's founders, who created an institution based on the principle that understanding and connecting with nature are necessary conditions for a well-lived life.

Since its founding, many NYBG people have become known and celebrated for their professional accomplishments. Many, many more have done and still do the essential work of the institution without fanfare or due credit. Anyone who enjoys even a moment at the Garden owes a debt of gratitude to the horticulturists past and present who have expertly tended its gardens, plant collections, and natural landscapes day after day since 1895. Their dedication to excellence is as inspiring as the results of their unsung labor.

I am grateful to Larry Lederman for generously sharing his talent and passion for photography and for being the catalyst for our collaborations. Without his support and encouragement, I never would have had this opportunity to share my perspective on the wonder that is the New York Botanical Garden.

Finally, and most emphatically, there's A. P., *my* raison d'être. Without her, there would be no joy at all.

—TODD A. FORREST

ISBN: 9781580936279

Library of Congress Control Number: 2024949284

Captions
Front cover: Daffodil Valley
Back cover: Bronx River
Page 1: Rock Garden
Page 2: Native Plant Garden
Page 3: Rock Garden
Page 4: Daffodil Valley
Page 5: Daffodil Hill
Page 6: Rock Garden
Page 8: Azalea Garden
Page 10: Bronx River Gorge. Mertz Library, NYBG

Design: Phil Kovacevich

Printed in China

Monacelli
A Phaidon Company
111 Broadway
New York, New York 10006